AFRIKA-STUDIEN Nr. 57

DEPARTMENT OF ECONOMICS, UNIVERSITY OF GHANA,
LEGON
IFO-INSTITUT FÜR WIRTSCHAFTSFORSCHUNG MÜNCHEN
AFRIKA-STUDIENSTELLE

Deficit Financing, Inflation and Capital Formation

The Ghanaian Experience 1960—65

by

NASEEM AHMAD

Senior Lecturer in Economics
University of Ghana

WELTFORUM VERLAG · MÜNCHEN

SPONSORED BY THE FRITZ THYSSEN-STIFTUNG, KÖLN

© by Weltforum-Verlag GmbH, München 1970
Library of Congress Catalog Card Number 74—143795
ISBN 3 8039 0042 5
Print: Druckerei G. J. Manz AG, Dillingen/Donau
Printed in Germany

Review of Published and Forthcoming Studies within the African Research Programme

The entire research programme being conducted up to June 1970 by the African Studies Centre of the Ifo Institute – partly by the Centre itself, partly in conjunction with other institutes and researchers – covers the studies listed below (see also introductory remarks in vols. 1 and 2 of "Afrika-Studien").

For readers' information on changes, supplements, and forthcoming publications, each volume of "Afrika-Studien" will contain a review of the programme as a whole.

Vols. 1–18 have been issued by Springer Publishing House, Berlin–Heidelberg–New York, subsequent volumes by Weltforum Publishing House, Munich, in co-operation with publishing houses in the United Kingdom and the United States. The studies published as mimeographs (African Research Reports) can be obtained through the African Studies Centre of the Ifo Institute for Economic Research (early editions only); the more recent editions (from 1968 onwards) are available through the Weltforum Publishing House, Munich.

A chronological list of published and forthcoming studies is attached at the end of this book.

General Economic Studies

a) Tropical Africa

N. Ahmad / E. Becher, Development Banks and Corporations in Tropical Africa (printed as volume 1), in German

R. Güsten / H. Helmschrott, National Accounting Systems in Tropical Africa (printed as volume 3), in German

N. Ahmad / E. Becher / E. Harder, Economic Planning and Development Policy in Tropical Africa (mimeograph), in German

H.-G. Geis, The Monetary and Banking Systems of the Countries of West Africa (printed as volume 20), in German

5

Africa-Vademecum (Basic Data on the Economic Structure and Development of Africa), prepared by F. BETZ (series Information and Documentation, vol. 1), in German, with additional headings in English and French

Development Aid to Africa, prepared by F. BETZ (series Information and Documentation, volume 3), in German

H. HARLANDER / D. MEZGER, Development Banks and Institutions in Africa (Series Information and Documentation, volume 2), in German

K. ERDMANN, Development Aid to Africa – with Special Reference to the Countries of East Africa (mimeograph), in German

H. AMANN, Operational Concepts of the Infrastructure in the Economic Development Process (mimeograph), in German

N. AHMAD, Deficit Financing, Inflation and Capital Formation. The Ghanaian Experience 1960–65 (printed as volume 57), in English

b) East Africa

L. SCHNITTGER, Taxation and Economic Development in East Africa (printed as volume 8), in German

R. GÜSTEN, Problems of Economic Growth and Planning: The Sudan Example (printed as volume 9), in English

P. v. MARLIN, The Impact of External Economic Relations on the Economic Development of East Africa (mimeograph), in English

R. VENTE, Planning Processes: The East African Case (printed as volume 52), in English

F. GOLL, Israeli Aid to Developing Countries with Special Reference to East Africa (mimeograph), in German

W. FISCHER, Problems of Land-Locked Countries: Uganda (printed as volume 41), in German

H. HIEBER, Economic Statistics in Developing Countries: The Example of Uganda (printed as volume 40), in German

G. HÜBNER, Importance, Volume, Forms and Development Possibilities of Private Saving in East Africa (mimeograph), in German

M. YAFFEY, Balance of Payments Problems in a Developing Country: Tanzania (printed as volume 47), in English

E.-J. PAUW, Money and Banking in East Africa (Kenya, Tanzania, Uganda) (printed as volume 35), in German

D. BALD, Administration and Economic Exploitation of German East Africa before 1914 (printed as volume 54), in German

M. Bohnet / H. Reichelt, Applied Research in East Africa and Its Influence on Economic Development (in preparation), in English

P. Marlin and Contributors, Financial Aspects of Development in East Africa (printed as volume 53), in English

Agricultural Studies

a) Tropical Africa

H. Klemm / P. v. Marlin, The EEC Market Regulations for Agricultural Products and Their Implications for Developing Countries (mimeograph), in German

H. Pössinger, Agricultural Development in Angola and Moçambique (printed as volume 31), in German

J. O. Müller, The Attitude of Various Tribes of the Republic of Togo, Especially the Ewe on the Plateau de Dayes, towards the Problem of Commissioned Cattle Herding by the Fulbe (Peulh) of West Africa (printed as volume 14 in German, mimeographed in French)

E.-S. El-Shagi, Reorganization of Land Use in Egypt (printed as volume 36), in German

H. Thorwart, Methods and Problems of Farm Management Surveys in Africa South of the Sahara (in preparation)

B. Mohr, Rice Cultivation in West Africa – A Presentation of the Economic and Geographical Differences of Cultivation Methods (printed as volume 44)

R. Bartha, Fodder Plants in the Sahel Zone of Africa (in German, English and French), (printed as volume 48)

b) East Africa

1. Basic Studies

H. Ruthenberg, Agricultural Development in Tanganyika (printed as volume 2), in English

H. Ruthenberg, African Agricultural Production Development Policy in Kenya 1952–1965 (printed as volume 10), in English

H. Dequin, Agricultural Development in Malawi (mimeograph), in English

H. Kraut/H.-D. Cremer (ed.), Investigations into Health and Nutrition in East Africa (printed as volume 42), in English

H. Blume, Organizational Aspects of Agro-Industrial Development Agencies – 9 Case Studies in Africa (Tea – Cotton – Oil-Palm) (being printed as volume 58), in English

2. Studies Concerning Grassland Use and Animal Husbandry in East Africa

H. Leippert, Botanical Investigations in the Masai Country/Tanzania (an Example from the Semi-Arid Areas of East Africa), (mimeograph), in German

H. Klemm, The Organization of Milk Markets in East Africa (mimeograph), in German

K. Meyn, Beef Production in East Africa (mimeograph), in English

H. Späth, Development Possibilities of the Pig and Poultry Industry in East Africa (in preparation)

Walter/Dennig, Comparative Investigations into the Efficiency of Utilizable Ruminants in Kenya (in preparation)

H. Jahnke/A. Matteucci, Trypanosomiasis among Humans and Animals in Africa — Measures of Control from an Economic Point of View (in preparation)

R. Bartha, Studies in Zebu Cattle Breeding in Tropical Africa (being printed as volume 59), in German

3. Studies in the Organization of Smallholder Farming in East Africa

D. v. Rotenhan, Land Use and Animal Husbandry in Sukumaland/Tanzania (printed as volume 11), in German

H. Pössinger, Investigations into the Productivity and Profitabilility of Smallholder Sisal in East Africa (printed as volume 13), in German

S. Groeneveld, Problems of Agricultural Development in the Coastal Region of East Africa (printed as volume 19), in German

V. Janssen, Agrarian Patterns in Ethiopia and their Implications for Economic Growth (in preparation), in German

H. Ruthenberg (ed.), Smallholder Farming and Smallholder Development in Tanzania – Ten Case Studies (printed as volume 24), in English

M. Attems, Smallholders in the Tropical Highlands of East Africa. The Usambara Mts. in the Transition Period from Subsistence to Market Production (printed as volume 25), in German

F. Scherer, Vegetable Cultivation in Tropical Highlands: The Kigezi Example (Uganda) (mimeograph), in English

v. Haugwitz/Thorwart, Farm Management Systems in Kenya (in preparation)

W. Scheffler, Smallholder Production under Close Supervision: Tobacco Growing in Tanzania. A Socio-Economic Study (printed as volume 27), in German

H. RABE, Crop Cultivation on the Island of Madagascar with Special Reference to Rice Growing (mimeograph)

E. BAUM, Traditional Farming and Land Development in the Kilombero Valley/Tanzania (mimeograph), in German

R. GOLKOWSKY, Irrigation in Kenya's Agriculture with Special Reference to the Mwea-Tebere Project (printed as volume 39), in German

H. PÖSSINGER, Problems and Structure of African Smallholder Coffee Plantations in the Highland of Angola (in preparation)

4. Other Studies Concerning Agricultural Development

M. PAULUS, The Role of Co-operatives in the Economic Development of East Africa, and Especially of Tanganyika and Uganda (printed as volume 15), in German

N. NEWIGER, Co-operative Farming in Kenya and Tanzania (mimeograph), in English

J. VASTHOFF, Small Farm Credit and Development – Some Experiences in East Africa with Special Reference to Kenya (printed as volume 33), in English

F. DIETERLEN / P. KUNKEL, Zoological Studies in the Kivu Region (Congo-Kinshasa) (mimeograph), in German

W. ERZ, Game Protection and Game Utilization in Rhodesia and in South Africa (mimeograph), in German

M. BARDELEBEN, Co-operatives in the Sudan: Their Characteristics, Functions and Suitability in the Socio-Economic Development Process (completed), in German

Studies in Commerce, Trade and Transport

H. HELMSCHROTT, Structure and Growth of the East African Textile and Garments Industry (printed as volume 45), in German

H. KAINZBAUER, Trade in Tanzania (printed as volume 18), in German

K. SCHÄDLER, Crafts and Small-Scale Industries in Tanzania (printed as volume 34), in English

K. SCHÄDLER, Manufacturing and Processing Industries in Tanzania (mimeograph), in English

H. REICHELT, The Chemical and Allied Industries in Kenya (mimeograph), in English

R. GÜSTEN, Studies in the Staple Food Economy of Western Nigeria (printed as volume 30), in English

9

G. W. Heinze, The Role of the Transport Sector in Development Policy – with Special Reference to African Countries – (printed as volume 21), in German

H. Amann, Energy Supply and Economic Development in East Africa (printed as volume 37)

R. Hofmeier, Problems of the Transport Economy in Tanzania with Special Reference to Road Transport (completed), in English (mimeographed in German)

P. Zajadacz and Contributors, Studies in Production and Trade in East Africa (printed as volume 51), in English

T. Möller, Mining and Regional Development in East Africa (in preparation)

H. Milbers, The Requirements for the Means of Transport in East Africa with a View to the Economic Expansion of these Countries (in preparation)

Sociological and Demographic Studies

A. Molnos, Attitudes towards Family Planning in East Africa (printed as volume 26), in English

O. Raum, The Human Factor in the Development of the Kilombero Valley (mimeograph), in English

O. Neuloh a. o., The African as Industrial Worker in East Africa (printed as volume 43), in German

H. W. Jürgens, Contributions to Internal Migration and Population Development in Liberia (printed as volume 4), in German

I. Rothermund, The Political and Economic Role of the Asian Minority in East Africa (printed as volume 6), in German

J. Jensen, Continuity and Change in the Division of Labour among the Baganda (Uganda) (printed as volume 17), in German

W. Clement, Applied Economics of Education – The Example of Senegal – (printed as volume 23), in German

H. W. Jürgens, Examination of the Physical Development of Tanzanian Youth (mimeograph), in English

H. W. Jürgens, Investigations into Internal Migration in Tanzania (printed as volume 29), in German

A. v. Gagern, The African Settlers and How They Organize Their Life in the Urambo-Scheme (Tanzania) (printed as volume 38), in German

Gerken / Schubert / Brandt, The Influence of Urbanization upon the Development of Rural Areas – with Special Reference to Jinja (Uganda) and Its Surroundings (in preparation)

E. C. KLEIN, Social Change in Kiteezi (Buganda), a Village within the Sphere of Influence of the Township of Kampala (Uganda) (printed as volume 46), in German

U. WEYL, Population Trends and Migration in Malawi with Special Reference to the Central Region of Lake Malawi (in preparation)

M. MECK, Population Trends in Kenya and Their Implications for Social Services in Rural and Urban Areas (in preparation)

STAEWEN/SCHÖNBERG, Cultural Change and Anxiety Reaction among the Yoruba of Nigeria (printed as volume 50), in German with English Summary

J. MURIUKI, The Mau-Mau Movement: Its Socio-Economic and Political Causes and Implications upon British Colonial Policy in Kenya and Africa (in preparation), in English

H. DESSELBERGER, Education's Contribution to Economic Development of a Tropical Agrarian Country – the Example of Tanzania (in preparation)

D. BERG-SCHLOSSER, The Distribution of Income and Education in Kenya: Causes and Potential Political Consequences (mimeograph), in English

Legal Studies

H. FLIEDNER, Land Tenure Reform in Kenya (printed as volume 7), in German

H. KRAUSS, Land Legislation in the Cameroons 1884–1964 (printed as volume 12), in German

G. SPREEN, The Present State of Legislation in East Africa (in preparation)

K. V. SPERBER, Public Administration in Tanzania (printed as volume 55), in English

F. V. BENDA-BECKMANN, Development of Law in Malawi (printed as volume 56), in German

Studies in Economic Geography

W. MARQUARDT, The Interrelationship between Man, Nature and Economy: the Example of Madagascar (in preparation)

H.-O. NEUHOFF, Gabun: History, Structure and Problems of the Export Trade of a Developing Country (printed as volume 16), in German

H. D. LUDWIG, Ukara: A Special Case of Land Use in the Tropics (printed as volume 22), in German

R. Jätzold/E. Baum, The Kilombero Valley/Tanzania: Characteristic Features of the Economic Geography of a Semihumid East African Flood Plain and Its Margins (printed as volume 28), in English

A. J. Halbach, The Economy of South West Africa (a Study in Economic Geography) (mimeograph), in German

J. A. Hellen, Rural Economic Development in Zambia 1890–1964 (printed as volume 32), in English

K. Engelhard, The Economico-Geographical Pattern of East Africa (in preparation)

J. Schultz, Iraqw Highland/Tanzania: Resource Analysis of an East African Highland and its Margins (in preparation)

K. Gerresheim, Evaluation of Aerial Photography in East Africa (an Inventory) (mimeograph), in German

W. Magura, Agricultural Development in the Bantu-Homelands of South and South-West Africa (completed), in German

H. Schiffers, The Sahara and its Margins. Characteristics of a large Natural Region (3 volumes, completed), in German

Bibliographies and Others

D. Mezger / E. Littich, Recent English Economic Research in East Africa. A Selected Bibliography (mimeograph), in German

A. Molnos, Annotated Bibliography of Social Research in East Africa 1954–1963 (printed as volume 5), in German

B. Heine, Status and Use of African Lingua Francas (printed as volume 49), in English

M. Bohnet, Science and Development Policy: The Problem of Applying Research Results (mimeograph), in German

Preface

The six-year period from 1960 to 1965 in Ghana was marked by conscious and intensive efforts by the Government to speed up economic development. No doubt, during these years the country achieved solid and impressive results in certain fields, notably education, power, transportation and industrialization. But these were also the years of growing financial instability, mounting prices, dwindling external reserves, and increasing disequilibrium in the balance of payments. As a result of growing emphasis on government investment in both infrastructural and directly productive projects, significant budget deficits emerged which were increasingly financed by borrowing from the banking system. The large doses of deficit financing during the period led to a rapid build up of unsatisfied aggregate demand, which kept domestic prices zooming and balance of payments gap widening, despite the introduction of price controls and the fairly strict import and foreign exchange restrictions. The inflationary pressures and balance of payments difficulties were no doubt compounded by a continuous fall in the cocoa prices in the world market. However, at the root of the severe economic and financial crisis which the country faced in 1966 was the fact that domestic output by and large failed to respond to the expansionary impulses generated by deficit financing in the government sector, partly due to the peculiar structure of the economy and partly due to the very nature and direction of government investment outlays. Consequently, even though the level of real capital formation increased appreciably, the rate of growth of the economy declined steadily. The paradoxical situation of 'investment without growth' which characterized the Ghanaian economy during the major part of the period under review culminated not only in the virtual exhaustion of large foreign exchange reserves and the accumulation of a huge external debt, but also in the severe shortages of essential commodities and the gradual fall in standards of living.

The present study attempts to review and analyze these and some related developments in Ghana in greater detail. Its main object is an evaluation of the experience of Ghana with money creation as a method of financing economic development. The focus is quite narrowly on the interrelation between deficit financing, inflationary process, capital formation and economic growth in a developing country during a relatively short period.

13

As the approach is a quantitative one, it must be emphasized that in developing the statistical picture of the economy and drawing various conclusions I have relied exclusively on the official data either published or directly available. Since for various reasons the data used in this study are far from perfect, the conclusions based on them necessarily suffer from certain limitations.

I am fully aware of the various gaps in the analysis and the rather cavalier treatment of a number of important issues. These are not due to any lack of interest on my part, but rather to absence of reliable data. Despite the ever increasing flow of statistical information released by various official agencies and the publication of a number of scholarly books and articles by various analysts, our knowledge of the economy of Ghana remains quite inadequate. Intensive studies of the various aspects of the economy are needed which may increase our understanding of its structure and behaviour. I do hope that the present study will serve to stimulate further research on the economy of Ghana by my learned and more capable colleagues both in and outside Legon.

The study is not exclusively designed for students of economics. Since the analysis developed is fairly simple, the book should also be of interest to the general reader who desires understanding of economic problems of developing countries. I would, however, feel satisfied if the book finds a place in the reading lists for students of economics in Ghana and elsewhere.

The study is the outgrowth of a research project undertaken during the period from September to December, 1967, when I was a Visiting Research Fellow at the Centre of West African Studies, University of Birmingham. I take this opportunity to record my thanks to the University of Ghana for granting me study leave for the period, and to the Director and Staff of the Centre of West African Studies for making my brief stay with them so rewarding and fruitful.

Earlier versions of part of this study were presented at staff seminar meetings at Birmingham and Legon in November 1967 and February 1968 respectively. To the participants at these seminars I am grateful for their helpful comments.

In addition, a large number of individuals and institutions have in one way or another helped me during the various stages of my research. I wish to express my deep gratitude to Douglas RIMMER of the Centre of West African Studies; Tony KILLICK, now a member of Harvard Advisory Group in Ghana; Reginald GREEN, now Economic Adviser to the Government of Tanzania; and Alex ASHIAGBOR of the Bank of Ghana. These knowledgeable colleagues went through the first draft, and offered extended and searching comments. I am also grateful to Professor T. M. BROWN of the University of Western Ontario, who during his recent association with the University of

Ghana spent considerable time in reading the entire manuscript and gave invaluable advice. In the preparation of the manuscript I have also benefited from many lively and stimulating discussions on various issues with my colleagues Jones OFORI-ATTA (now Ministerial Secretary to the Ministry of Finance and Economic Planning), Joe ABBEY and James ABBAN. I am also indebted to my friend and former colleague Jitendra MOHAN, now a Lecturer in Political Science at the University of Sheffield, who went through the first two chapters of the manuscript with great care and saved the text from numerous blemishes of expression and style. I must in addition acknowledge a heavy debt of gratitude to Professor Z. L. SADOWSKI, the former Head of Economics Department and Dean of the Faculty of Social Studies, University of Ghana, without whose inspiring encouragement and constructive comments the study would not have taken the shape it has.

I should also like to thank Mr. S. W. K. SOSUH of the Central Bureau of Statistics and Mr. M. T. AMOAKO-ATTA of the Bank of Ghana for their substantial help in securing unpublished fiscal and monetary data from their respective institutions.

The heavy burden of typing and retyping of the manuscript was borne largely by Mr. B. K. FREEMAN with some assistance from Mr. G. T. ADJABENG. They both deserve my thanks for their assiduous assistance.

Thanks are also due to Dr. Wilhelm MARQUARDT for showing interest in the publication of the present study, to Mr. Axel J. HALBACH for undertaking the arduous task of supervising its publication, and to the Fritz-Thyssen Foundation, Cologne, for making the publication possible by a generous financial support.

A final word of deepest gratitude is due to my wife, whose untiring understanding and devotion enabled me to maintain my morale during the crucial stages of work. The book is dedicated to her.

Department of Economics,   Naseem AHMAD
University of Ghana,
Legon,
August, 1970.

Contents

List of Text Tables

List of Appendix Tables

Note on Currency Equivalents

Prior to July 19, 1965, the Ghana pound (£G) was the currency in circulation in Ghana. The external value of the Ghana pound, established initially on November 5, 1958, was:

$$£G1 = US\$2.80$$
$$US\$1 = £G0.357$$

The external value of the Ghana pound was, therefore, at par with the pound sterling.

On July 19, 1965, a decimal currency unit, known as cedi (₵) was introduced to replace the Ghana pound. The conversion rate between the cedi and the Ghana pound was fixed at:

$$₵1 = £G0.417 \text{ (i.e., 8s.4d.)}$$
$$£G1 = ₵2.40$$

The external value of the cedi was established at:

$$₵1 = US\$1.166$$
$$US\$1 = ₵0.857$$

Thus, decimalization of the monetary system was not accompanied by a change in the external value of the Ghana currency. The Ghana pound continued to be legal tender until September 17, 1966, and was not formally demonetized until December 17, 1966.

During the period of change-over the new monetary system was strongly criticized by certain sections of the population, mainly on the ground that the conversion rate between the cedi and the Ghana pound was "awkward" and "inconvenient". Although the arguments against it were by no means convincing, some time after the coup it was decided to change the basis of the currency unit from 8s.4d. to 10s.

On February 23, 1967, i.e., a year after the coup, a new currency, known as the new cedi (N₵) was introduced to replace the old cedi. The conversion rate between the new and the old currency unit was established at:

$$N₵1 = ₵1.20$$
$$₵1 = N₵0.833$$

The external value of the new cedi was fixed at:

$$N\mathbb{C}1 = US\$1.40$$
$$US\$1 = N\mathbb{C}0.714$$

Once again, the change in the monetary system did not lead to a revaluation of the currency.

On July 8, 1967, the new cedi was effectively devalued. Since then the par value of the new cedi stands at[*]:

$$N\mathbb{C}1 = US\$0.98$$
$$US\$1 = N\mathbb{C}1.02$$

Throughout the present study the values are given in the Ghana pound. This has been done deliberately, because the study relates to a period when the Ghana pound was in effective circulation. Those who insist on being up-to-date in matters of currency, can do so by simply doubling the data presented here.

---

[*] On November 18, 1967, when the par value of the pound sterling was reduced from US\$2.80 to US\$2.40, Ghana like many other Sterling Area countries did not devalue her currency. Since then, the rate of exchange between the new cedi and the pound sterling stands at N$\mathbb{C}$ 1 = £0.408 sterling or £1 sterling = N$\mathbb{C}$ 2.45.

Chapter I

DEFICIT FINANCING IN GHANA, 1960—65: ITS NATURE AND EXTENT

1. Introduction

National governments in the developing countries are today faced with a formidable task: on the one hand, despite the differences in their ideological orientation and political set-up, they have chosen to spend huge sums not only on the improvement of infrastructure but, in view of the absence or lethargy of private enterprise, on the development of superstructure as well; on the other hand, a large variety of social, economic and administrative factors tend to restrict the growth of revenue from taxation. Moreover, at least in the initial stages, the gap between government expenditures and revenues often gets wider since completion of infrastructure projects invariably leads to an immediate increase in recurrent expenditures but does not for quite some time add anything to revenues. In principle, there is always some scope for cutting down non-development expenditures, especially on civil administration and defence and to devoting an increasing share of national resources to development projects. In practice, however, it is often difficult to switch over to a stringent economy, partly because 'independence is expensive' in the sense that it immediately calls for new financial commitments (diplomatic representation abroad, membership of international organizations, etc.), and partly because expenditures on civil administration and defence, once raised to certain levels, create strong vested interests, which cannot be easily ignored.

In view of the growing imbalance between their revenues and expenditures, the governments in the developing countries have been obliged to solicit foreign capital. In addition to providing the much needed foreign exchange for the import of capital goods, capital from abroad very often brings with it the technology, the experience in management as well as the links with international markets. In these and similar respects foreign loans and investments can be helpful in accelerating the pace of economic development in the developing countries.

21

The role of foreign capital in economic development can, however, be easily misconceived and exaggerated. The case for foreign capital is that it can operate as a catalytic agent making it possible to harness domestic resources. But foreign capital, no matter how large the inflow, cannot absolve a recipient country from the task of mobilizing domestic resources. The economic history of most of the developed countries as well as the experience of the developing countries in recent years affirm the view that, despite its important role in promoting economic development, foreign capital alone cannot create any permanent basis for higher standards of living in the future. Foreign capital can relieve initial foreign exchange shortages, stimulate domestic production and increase domestic incomes, but to ensure self-sustained economic growth it is necessary to generate domestic savings, to mobilize them effectively and to canalize them into productive investments.

The task of mobilizing domestic resources for economic development has become all the more urgent because in recent years the developing countries have found it increasingly difficult to obtain sufficient external capital at reasonably favourable terms and conditions. In the first place, the rate of increase in the total flow of resources from the developed to the developing countries has been disappointingly slow [1]. Secondly, in recent years there has been a discernible change in the sources and terms of foreign credits and investments: while in the 1950's official 'aid' at concessional terms constituted the main source of flow of external resources, of late the developing countries

---

1 According to the estimates prepared by the Organization for Economic Co-operation and Development (O.E.C.D.), the total flow of resources to the developing countries (including certain European countries like Greece, Spain and Yugoslavia) from all sources, viz. the O.E.C.D. member nations, other industrial countries, Sino-Soviet bloc countries and the multilateral organizations (IBRD, IDA, IFC, etc.) increased from some $8,000 million in 1960 to approximately $9,000 million in 1961, $10,000 million in 1964 and $11,000 in 1965. These figures include direct bilateral contributions, including technical assistance from donor nations, grants and loans from the multilateral agencies and private investments, including reinvested earnings. The data are 'net' in the sense that return flows in the form of amortization payments as well as the repatriation of capital by residents of donor countries are deducted.

Note, however, that these estimates are primarily based on the information supplied by the donor countries. It is quite likely that at least some of the items included in the estimates were commitments and not actual disbursements. Moreover, the data are in current dollar value; they do not take into account the increase in prices of aid-financed goods and services from donor countries, nor have they been adjusted for the effects of decline in the unit value of exports of recipient countries on the volume of their exports required to finance debt service. It is evident that at least a part of this increase in the flow of resources to the developing countries was offset by the price movements. Consequently, the real value of aid may in fact not have increased to any significant extent. See, O.E.C.D.: *The Inflow of Financial Resources to Less-Developed Countries, 1961–65*, Paris, 1967.

have been forced to rely more and more on private foreign capital at conventional terms. Available studies of the flow of foreign capital to the developing countries indicate that in recent years the amount of official transfers has tended to stagnate[2]. What is worse, the stagnation in the flow of official capital has been accompanied by an increasing resort to 'aid tying' whereby a donor country requires that the funds provided by it are spent on buying its own goods and services[3]. 'Aid tying' discourages international bidding procedures for the award of contracts and "in general it is reckoned that a tied grant or loan ... may reduce the value of the aid by as much as 20 per cent"[4].

The situation with regard to private foreign capital is not very different. It is true that the flow of private foreign capital has shown some increase in recent years, but the increase has been neither continuous nor spectacular[5]. Furthermore, private foreign capital is generally available at terms and conditions which are not always in the best interest of the recipient countries. Thus, even if no other 'strings' are attached, private foreign loans are often available either at considerably high rates of interest or for relatively short durations or for projects of little or no importance to the national economies of the developing countries.

Urgent and ever-increasing need for stepping-up the level of development expenditure on the one hand, and the great difficulties in mobilizing domestic resources through the normal means of taxation and internal borrowing as well as the despair and disillusionment over the flow of foreign capital, on the other, have forced the governments in many developing countries to cover their budgetary gaps by deficit financing or money creation. Resort to deficit financing as a means of mobilizing resources for economic development has of late become so widespread that, despite the inherent dangers of inflation and balance of payments disequilibrium, it is now generally considered as an essential and unavoidable tool for accelerating the rate of real capital formation.

2. Scope of the Study

This study seeks to analyze the extent and impact of monetary expansion in Ghana during the years 1960–65 with special reference to the deficit financing

---

2 For instance, in the period from 1961 to 1965 there was hardly any increase in total official net disbursements by the O.E.C.D. member nations. *Ibid.*, p. 23.

3 It is difficult to define the term 'aid tying' in any precise manner since the conditions imposed by the donor countries vary widely. For further details of conditions imposed by the donor countries, *see, ibid.*, pp. 110–114.

4 U. K. HICKS: *Development Finance – Planning and Control*, Oxford University Press, 1965, p. 39.

5 O.E.C.D., *op. cit.*, table II.I., p. 24.

in the government sector[6]. The six-year period with which we shall be concerned represents an important phase in the economic history of Ghana from the viewpoint of development efforts as well as the resort to deficit financing. Only with the launching of the *Second Five-Year Plan*, 1959/64, in March 1959, did independent Ghana enter the arena of conscious efforts for economic development. The development efforts gained momentum in 1960 when government capital expenditure was increased substantially[7]. The year 1960 also marked the beginning of an uninterrupted series of sizeable budget deficits as well as the use of money creation as an instrument of financing these deficits. Although the *Second Five-Year Plan* was in the closing months of 1961 officially discarded[8], government capital expenditure continued to run at a high level in the ensuing period. The introduction of the *Seven-year Development Plan*, 1963/70, in 1964 led to further considerable jumps in government outlays with the result that during 1965 deficit financing rose to an alarmingly high level. This phase of rapid growth in government spending, huge budget deficits and extensive resort to money creation came to an end in February 1966, when a new regime came to power and in an effort to stabilize the economy took firm measures to control government expenditure, reduce the size of budget deficit and check the rate of deficit financing. The new regime imposed strict financial controls on the ministries and departments, cancelled the implementation of uneconomic projects, confined its capital expenditure to the on-going projects and placed tight ceilings on government borrowing from the banking system.

Two major questions with which we shall be concerned in this study are the impact of deficit financing by the Government on the inflationary situation in the country and on the level of real capital formation. It has been frequently argued that in a developing country where the taxation base is narrow and the level of voluntary savings low, deficit financing can be helpful in detaching national resources from their conventional uses and diverting them into productive channels. In other words, it is often claimed that by resorting to money creation the government in a developing country can extract additional savings from the population and consequently speed-up the rate of real investment. Advocates of deficit financing therefore believe that inasmuch as deficit financing encourages real capital formation, its adverse social and economic consequences via inflation and balance of payments disequilibrium

6 In this study, the terms 'government sector' and 'government' when used in the Ghanaian context mean the Central Government of Ghana. The reasons for this narrow definition of government sector are explained in chapter III.

7 *See*, appendix table XIV.

8 No official explanation was ever given for the decision to abandon the Plan. E. N. OMABOE has, however, put forward a number of possible explanations. *See*, W. BIRMINGHAM, I. NEUSTADT, E. N. OMABOE (eds.): *A Study of Contemporary Ghana, Volume One – The Economy of Ghana*, George Allen and Unwin, 1966, pp. 450–452.

ought to be looked at and tolerated as a necessary price for economic development and growth. An overall appraisal of these arguments in the Ghanaian context is the main purpose of this study.

To bring out some of the salient features of the impact of government deficit finance operations on the inflationary pressures, the balance of payments, the rate of real capital formation and the rate of real growth, the six-year period under review can be conveniently divided into the following three sub-periods of two years each:

- 1960–61, when the *Second Five-Year Plan* was in operation and, at least to some extent, provided a basis for the pace and pattern of government development efforts;
- 1962–63, when no development plan existed and the projects were initiated and implemented on an *ad hoc* basis; and
- 1964–65, when with the launching of the *Seven-Year Development Plan* the efforts for accelerating the pace of economic development became more conscious and concerted[9].

Although, as already mentioned, government spending continued to increase uninterruptedly throughout the six-year period, it has been found useful to distinguish between the plan-periods and the no-plan-period in order to analyse the extent, if any, to which economic planning as a policy variable influenced the level of money creation and the manner in which the economy responded to the expansionary impulse generated by the government deficit finance operations.

3. Concepts of Deficit Financing

Our first task is to choose a suitable concept of deficit financing for the purpose of the present study. The need for this choice arises because a number of definitions of the term are in circulation. Not only are there considerable differences in the connotations given to the term in various countries, but also different writers have used different measures of deficit financing for their analyses.

Deficit financing is often identified with budget deficit. This, however, is a very vague definition of deficit financing because there is no universally acceptable concept of budget deficit and the meaning of the term differs from one country to another. Thus, for example, whereas in the United Kingdom the term budget deficit denotes the excess of current expenditure over current

---

9 As in many other developing countries, the publication of the *Seven-Year Development Plan* in Ghana was delayed by about six months and the Plan was formally launched in early 1964. For the purpose of this study, 1964 is considered as the first year of the *Seven-Year Development Plan*.

revenue, i.e., deficit on current account only, in the United States it generally refers to the gap between total budgetary expenditure (both on current and capital accounts), and current revenue, i.e., over-all budget deficit[10].

A more serious demerit of the above definition of deficit financing is that it is not helpful in analysing the economic effects of government fiscal operations. It does not, for instance, indicate whether a budget deficit has resulted from an increase in government expenditure or from a decrease in taxation. Nor does it shed any light on the method (or methods) used to finance such a deficit. Since the impact of a budget deficit on aggregate demand in the economy will differ both according to the way it is 'created' and the source from which it is financed[11], its size by itself gives little, if any, indication of whether government fiscal operations would generate expansionary or contractionary trends.

Since in this study we shall be concerned, *inter alia,* with the inflationary pressures attendant upon government fiscal operations, it is necessary to define deficit financing in terms of those methods of covering budgetary gaps which have a tendency to increase aggregate expenditure in the economy[12]. A budget deficit, once created, can be financed in one or more of the following methods: a) running down of cash balances; b) borrowing from the central bank; c) borrowing from the commercial banks; and, d) borrowing from the 'public', i.e., non-bank institutions (savings banks, insurance companies, trusts, pension funds, local bodies, business firms, etc.) and individuals[13].

It has been frequently argued that government borrowing from the 'public' does not usually lead to any net increase in aggregate demand in the economy. This argument is based on the assumption that government borrowing from the 'public' represents a withdrawal of funds which might otherwise have been either spent on consumer goods and services or invested in private

---

10 In Ghana, government current revenue never fell short of current expenditure. The term budget deficit therefore denotes much the same in Ghana as that in the United States.

11 For an illuminating analysis of the differences in economic effects of alternative methods of deficit 'creation' and financing, *see,* J. M. BUCHANAN: *The Public Finances,* Richard D. Irwin, Inc., Illinois, 1965, ch. 8.

12 Strictly speaking, the various methods of creating budget deficits should also be taken into account. Needless to say, this can be done only at the cost of added complexities. Another reason for confining our analysis to the sources of financing budget deficits is that on the whole aggregate demand is "influenced more by the means of financing than by the means of creating the deficit." *Ibid.,* p. 97.

13 Another possible means of financing budget deficit is to print currency (and deposit it with the central bank). This method is, however, seldom employed because the same results can be easily obtained by borrowing from the central bank. LERNER, however, argues that under certain circumstances the effects of printing additional currency and borrowing from the central bank may not be identical. *Cf.* A. P. LERNER: *Economics of Employment,* McGraw–Hill, New York, 1951, pp. 7–11 and 271–272.

earning assets so that a budget deficit so financed does not generate any expansion in the income-spending flow [14]. From the viewpoint of its macroeconomic effects, it is therefore customary to treat government borrowing from the 'public' as being similar to revenue from taxation. In other words, government borrowing from the 'public' is generally excluded from the measurement of money-creating effects of government fiscal operations [15].

This leaves us with the first three methods of financing budget deficit. Decline in government cash balances and government borrowing from the central bank are essentially inflationary means of financing in the sense that they *per se* increase the money supply in an economy [16]. Since the net money-creating effects of these two methods of financing are normally precisely equivalent, they are frequently lumped together. In contrast, in respect of its net money-creating effects, government borrowing from commercial banks is somewhat of a 'hybrid'; it may or may not lead to an increase in the money supply, depending upon, among other things, whether or not the commercial banks have excess 'primary' reserves.

Two concepts of deficit financing emerge from the above analysis. First, deficit financing is the net borrowing of the government from the central

---

14 Strictly speaking, this assumption is not always valid. For in a developing country like Ghana where hoarding of currency is quite widespread, government borrowing from individuals, especially if it is compulsory, can lead to an activation of money hoards with the result that there may be no reduction in private spending. The macroeconomic effects of hoarding function in a developing country are discussed in detail in chapter II.

15 Note, however, that while in the United States (and in many other countries including Ghana) for the purpose of measuring budget deficit government borrowing from the 'public' is excluded from current revenue, in India borrowing from the 'public' is treated on the same footing as revenue from taxation and therefore included in the measurement of budget deficit. In other words, the Indian concept of budget deficit is more narrow than the one used in the United States. Consequently, in the United States the term deficit financing is usually given a broader connotation than in India. *Cf.* R. J. CHELLIAH: *Fiscal Policy in Underdeveloped Countries*, George Allen & Unwin, London, 1960, p. 150.

16 BUCHANAN objects strongly to the use of the term 'borrowing' to denote the sale of government securities to the central bank. According to him, this form of financing "is precisely equivalent ... to the printing of fresh new currency to meet government expenditures in excess of tax revenues" and "should not therefore be included under the rubric 'borrowing' at all". Likewise, he disapproves of the widespread practice of denoting the sale of government securities to the commercial banks as 'borrowing' and argues that this operation can be labelled as 'borrowing' "only in some rather limited definitional sense". According to him, "the sale of government securities to the commercial banks can represent a genuine borrowing operation if funds are withdrawn from alternative bank investments". In this case, "no differential addition to the total money supply need take place". J. M. BUCHANAN: *op. cit.*, pp. 97–101.

bank (including decline in government cash balances)[17]. Second, deficit financing is the net borrowing of the government from the banking system, i.e., from the central bank as well as from the commercial banks[18]. According to these definitions, deficit financing is equivalent to that part of the budget deficit which has a bearing – direct or indirect – on the money supply in the economy. From the analytical point of view, the chief merit of these definitions is that they focus attention on those means of financing budget deficit which are potentially expansionary and thus make it easier to measure and examine the inflationary impact of government operations on the economy.

4. The Criterion for Choice

This brings us to the question of which of the two definitions of deficit financing given above is better or more useful. It seems that there is no simple or clearly defined answer to this question. The choice involved is essentially between whether or not, for the purpose of measurement and analysis of the expansionary impact of budget deficits on the economy, government borrowing from the commercial banks should be treated identically with borrowing from the central bank. The decision should obviously depend upon whether or not in a given situation government borrowing from the commercial banks has any net money-creating effect in the economy.

In the past there has been quite a controversy over the monetary effects of government borrowing from the central bank and the commercial banks. Today, the general consensus is that the inflationary consequences of the two sources of financing are not always identical. Note, for instance, that whereas government borrowing from the central bank enlarges the fiduciary issue and thereby tends to increase the stock of currency in the economy, borrowing from the commercial banks cannot. Again, whereas government borrowing from the central bank, coupled with the expenditure of these funds on the purchase of goods and services from the rest of the economy, provides the commercial banks with excess 'primary' reserves (i.e., cash balances and deposits with the central bank) and thereby tends to increase their potential capacity for making additional loans on a multiple basis[19], the expansionary

---

17 Henceforth in this study the term 'net borrowing from the central bank' is denoted to include decrease in government cash balances.

18 The first definition is much the same as that used in India's Five-Year Plans, whereas the second definition is identical with the one employed by the Pakistan Planning Commission. Cf. *The Second Five-Year Plan*, Government of India, 1956, p. 84, and *The Second Five-Year Plan (1960–65)*, Government of Pakistan, June 1960, p. 61.

19 In a fractional reserve banking system the credit multiplier (i.e., the potential credit-creation coefficient) will be equal to the reciprocal of $c + r - rc$, where c is the ratio of currency in circulation to money supply and r is the customary

effects of government borrowing from the commercial banks would depend upon a variety of factors, including whether or not the commercial banks have excess 'primary' reserves, the mechanism of government borrowing, and the extent, if any, to which the monetary authorities are willing to let these effects take place. Thus, for instance, government borrowing from the commercial banks may not have any net money-creating effect if:

- the commercial banks are without any excess 'primary' reserves, i.e., their cash balances and deposits with the central bank do not exceed the customary or legal reserves requirements;
- government borrowing from the commercial banks does not lead to an increase in their liquid assets, i.e., it takes the form of permanent or quasi-permanent debt; and,
- the central bank is either unwilling or unable to accommodate the commercial banks against the collateral of their holdings of government securities.

Under these conditions, an increase in government borrowing from the commercial banks is unlikely to generate inflationary trends in the economy. This is because, in such a situation, the commercial banks can increase their lending to the government either by disposing of some of their investment in private earning assets or by reducing their loans and advances to the non-government sector. In either case, an increase in the commercial banks' credit to the government will be offset by a decrease in their credit to the rest of the economy. In other words, under the circumstances outlined above, government borrowing from the commercial banks will be akin to borrowing from the 'public' in the sense that its expansionary effect on total outlay in the economy will be negligible. In this case, therefore, the first definition of deficit financing (net increase in government borrowing from the central bank) will be more appropriate than the second.

On the other hand, when either the commercial banks have excess 'primary' reserves and utilize these to buy government securities[20], or government borrowing takes a form which increases commercial banks' liquidity (e.g. sale of treasury bills), or the central bank stands ready to lend to the commercial banks, the second definition (net increase in government borrowing from the banking system) is more relevant than the first. For, in these circumstances, an increase in government borrowing from the commercial banks

---

or legal cash reserves ratio (i.e., the proportion of deposits kept by the commercial banks in the form of cash and deposits with the central bank).

20 This latter qualification is necessary because there is no assurance that the commercial banks will be always willing to utilize their excess reserves to buy government securities. For example, if the rate of interest offered by the government is relatively low, the commercial banks may not be very anxious to exchange their idle funds for government securities.

will necessarily activate funds which were hitherto idle and thus cause an expansion in the income-expenditure flow. Moreover, to the extent that government borrowing from the commercial banks injects additional liquidity into the banking system, it will make the money-credit system more elastic than before and thereby pave the way for an increase in the money supply on a multiple basis [21].

The conclusion emerging from the above analysis is that the inflationary effect of government borrowing from the commercial banks will depend upon the circumstances under which this transaction takes place. This in turn means that for the purpose of monetary analysis the choice between the two definitions of deficit financing should be made in the light of the statistical data on the response of the banking system to government borrowing operations.

5. Choice of the Concept Relevant to Ghana

We may now apply the above analytical technique to the case of Ghana with a view to determine which of the two concepts of deficit financing is more relevant to the present study. To this end, we shall make use of the data given in tables 1 and 2.

Table 1 shows the expansion and the changes in the composition of the commercial banks' assets during the six-year period under review. It can be seen from the table that while the total value of the commercial banks' assets went up from £G41.4 million in 1960 to £G121.0 million in 1965, the assets structure also changed significantly. To begin with, the commercial banks' holding of government paper (treasury bills and stocks) increased consistently from £G4.4 million in 1960 to £G43.6 million in 1965. Note, however, that until 1962 this increase emanated almost exclusively from the acquisition of short-term government paper, the Ghana Government Treasury Bills [22].

---

21 It is sometimes suggested that the expansionary effect of government borrowing from the commercial banks out of their excess reserves will normally remain limited to the initial and direct increase in income-expenditure flow and that despite an increase in elasticity of the money-credit system the commercial banks' lending to the non-government sector will not increase to any significant extent. This view is based on the argument that the very fact that prior to government borrowing the commercial banks possess excess 'primary' reserves indicates that there is a lack of demand for loans from the non-government sector. Needless to say, this argument is based on a static view of the economy and ignores the vital fact that increased government activity in a developing country can indirectly encourage private investment in commerce, agriculture and industry, etc., and thus raise the demand for credit-worthy loans from the commercial banks.

22 The Ghana Government Treasury Bills were for the first time introduced in February, 1960. Until then, the commercial banks used to invest their short-term funds in foreign (U.K. Government) treasury bills. The introduction of domestic

Table 1. Assets of the Commercial Banks, 1960–65

(Averages of End-of-Month Figures)

(₤G million and Percentages)

Assets	1960		1961		1962		1963		1964		1965	
Cash in hand	2.8	*(7)*	2.7	*(6)*	4.1	*(7)*	3.7	*(5)*	4.1	*(4)*	5.0	*(4)*
Balances with the Bank of Ghana	1.9	*(5)*	1.7	*(4)*	3.1	*(5)*	1.6	*(2)*	4.7	*(5)*	6.0	*(5)*
Balances with other banks	11.6	*(28)*	5.7	*(12)*	1.6	*(2)*	2.7	*(4)*	2.0	*(2)*	2.0	*(2)*
Ghana Government Treasury Bills	4.2	*(10)*	5.8	*(12)*	17.3	*(27)*	17.8	*(25)*	18.8	*(21)*	29.7	*(25)*
Other Bills	2.6	*(6)*	3.0	*(7)*	0.5	*(1)*	2.2	*(3)*	4.6	*(5)*	11.3	*(9)*
Total Liquid Assets	23.1	*(56)*	18.9	*(41)*	26.6	*(42)*	28.0	*(39)*	34.2	*(37)*	54.0	*(45)*
Ghana Government securities	0.2	*(1)*	0.6	*(1)*	1.1	*(2)*	5.5	*(8)*	12.6	*(14)*	13.9	*(11)*
Loans and advances	13.3	*(32)*	21.1	*(45)*	24.5	*(39)*	30.8	*(43)*	33.4	*(37)*	40.3	*(33)*
Other Assets	4.7	*(11)*	5.9	*(13)*	11.0	*(17)*	7.5	*(10)*	11.1	*(12)*	12.8	*(11)*
Total Assets	41.4	*(100)*	46.6	*(100)*	63.3	*(100)*	71.9	*(100)*	91.3	*(100)*	121.0	*(100)*

N.B.: Figures in brackets are percentages.

Sources: Statistical Year Book, 1963, table 146, p. 151.
Bank of Ghana Report, June 1965, table 6, pp. 102–103.
Bank of Ghana Report, June 1967, table 3, pp. 38–39.

Between 1960 and 1962 the Commercial banks' portfolio of the domestic treasury bills went up from £G4.2 million to £G17.3 million. In contrast, during the same period the volume of other liquid assets went down from £G18.9 million to £G9.3 million. The main contributory factor towards the decline in the volume of other liquid assets was the sharp fall in the balances with other banks, which comprised mainly the idle funds maintained by the expatriate commercial banks with their head offices in London and which, on the request of the Bank of Ghana, were repatriated [23].

The decline in the other liquid assets at first led to a significant fall in the volume of total liquid assets, from £G23.1 million in 1960 to £G18.9 million in 1961, with the consequence that the cash and liquidity ratios fell respectively from 33 and 53% to 21 and 43% (table 2). The downtrend in the commercial banks' liquidity in 1961 is explained by the fact that the brisk commercial activity in that year raised the demand for loans and advances, and induced by the higher rate of interest which such credits offered, the banks utilized a large part of the repatriated foreign balances for expanding their lending to the commercial sector [24]. Indeed, so high was the demand for loans and advances and so anxious were the commercial banks to make use of this opportunity that they even did not hesitate to rediscount a part of their domestic treasury bills' holdings with the Bank of Ghana [25]. Consequently, the commercial banks loans and advances went up from £G13.3 million per month in 1960 to £G21.1 million in 1961, an increase of about 60%.

During 1962 the commercial banks' overall liquidity position showed a considerable improvement. Despite a considerable decline in the volume of cash reserves (from £G10.1 million in 1961 to £G8.8 million in 1962) and the consequent fall in the cash ratio (from 21 to 15%), the volume of total liquid assets went up to £G26.6 million pushing up the liquidity ratio to 51%.

---

treasury bills led to a rapid decrease in the banks' holding of foreign treasury bills, and by the end of 1960 the commercial banks had completely run down their portfolio of foreign treasury bill. See, Bank of Ghana Report, June 1961, p. 21.

23 In compliance with the Exchange Control Regulations introduced in July, 1961, the Bank of Ghana requested the commercial banks to maintain outside Ghana only such balances as were necessary for the day-to-day transactions.

24 Credit to the commercial sector earned as much as 6 to 9% per annum, whereas the discount rate on 90-days treasury bills was around 4.5%. Cf. Bank of Ghana Report, June 1963, p. 59.

25 This was the first time the commercial banks resorted to this method of borrowing from the Bank of Ghana. Very soon, however, rediscounting of treasury bills became an almost normal feature of the commercial banks' operations, especially in the first and last quarters of the year when the demand for loan and advances is relatively higher than in the second and third quarters. Cf. Bank of Ghana Report, June 1961, p. 21, and Bank of Ghana Report, June 1963, p. 59.

Table 2. **Commercial Banks' Liquidity Position, 1960—65**
(Averages of End-of-Month Figures)
(Ratio to Deposits [a])

	1960	1961	1962	1963	1964 [b]	1965 [c]
a) Cash Reserves [d]	33	21	15	8	11	11
b) Other Liquid Reserves [e]	20	22	36	33	56	51
c) Total Liquid Reserves (a + b)	53	43	51	41	67	62
d) Special Deposits ('B' Account) with the Bank of Ghana	–	–	–	–	3	3
e) Ghana Government Securities	1	1	2	9	17	17
f) Total Reserves (c + d + e)	54	44	53	50	87	82

[a] From May 1964 on, excluding special mandatory deposits of 15% required prior to opening of letters of credit in respect of imports.

[b] Average of Wednesday figures for the nine months' period from April to December.

[c] Average of Wednesday figures for the period from January to December.

[d] Up to 1963 includes the following items: cash in tills, balances with the Bank of Ghana and net balances with other banks in Ghana and abroad.
From the year 1964 on, includes cash in tills, current account deposits with the Bank of Ghana and net balances with other banks in Ghana.

[e] Up to 1963 includes Ghana Government Treasury Bills, and other domestic and foreign bills. From April 1964 on, includes Ghana Government Treasury Bills, approved industrial and agricultural loans, and balances in special deposit ('L' Account) with the Bank of Ghana.

N.B. For further details of reserves requirements under the Credit Control Regulations introduced in April, 1964, *see,* appendix table X.

Sources: Statistical Year Book, 1963, table 146, p. 151.
Bank of Ghana Report, June 1966, table 5, p. 50.
Bank of Ghana Report, June 1967, table 4, p. 40.

As can be seen from table 1, this improvement in the liquidity position of the commercial banks in 1962 resulted from the sharp increase in their portfolio of domestic treasury bills, which between 1961 and 1962 went up by three-fold.

The significant increase in the commercial banks' holding of domestic treasury bills in 1962 was a by-product of the imposition of a series of restrictions on imports and transfer of capital and the introduction of an "austerity" budget in July 1961. These measures were aimed mainly at reducing consumer disposable incomes and arresting the deterioration in the country's balance of payments position. They inevitably led to some slackening in commercial activity during 1962 resulting in a fall in the demand for fresh loans and advances by the non-government sector. As a result, domestic treasury bills became the main avenue for the commercial banks' short-term investments. Note, however, that the increase in the commercial banks' holding of treasury bills did not lead to a decrease in their lending to the non-government sector. In fact, although the share of loans and advances in total assets fell from 45% in 1961 to 39% in 1962, the absolute level of these credits went up by £G3.4 million.

It is clear from the foregoing discussion that up to 1962 government borrowing from the commercial banks was mainly in the form of treasury bills, which the commercial banks acquired largely by repatriating their external balances and by running down their portfolio of foreign treasury bills. The commercial banks treated domestic treasury bills as their secondary reserves, and, as and when the demand for loans and advances in the non-government sector increased, rediscounted them with the Bank of Ghana at the current discount rate[26]. It is also evident that, despite a considerable shift in the composition of their liquid assets from external to internal ones and from cash reserves to other liquid assets, the commercial banks' potential capacity for credit expansion remained high. Consequently, up to 1962 their increased lending to the Government did not in any way prevent the commercial banks from expanding their credit to the non-government sector.

Thus, up to 1962 government borrowing from the commercial banks followed a pattern which tended to inject additional liquidity into the system. It is, however, by no means clear whether or not this was done in the hope that the commercial banks would hoard this liquidity and would not therefore expand their credit to the rest of the economy. Whatever the Government's intentions and expectations might have been, it is clear that the commercial banks on their part were not always willing to hoard liquidity. For, as we have already seen, when in 1961 the tempo of commercial activity rose, offering the commercial banks worthwhile alternative investment opportu-

---

26 In this exercise the commercial banks were also encouraged by the fact that there is no penal rate in Ghana.

nities, they did expand their credit to the non-government sector. Although, despite a significant increase in the commercial banks' holding of treasury bills, the situation in 1962 did not become explosive, the danger continued to exist.

It seems that during 1963 the Government became conscious of the danger inherent in the very nature of its borrowing operations and thus decided to reduce the liquidity of the banking system. This action took the form of funding £G10 million worth of treasury bill holding of the commercial banks into medium-term investment, the Conversion Stock 1967–68 [27].

The decision to withdraw liquidity from the banking system was a sound one. But, judging from its ultimate effect, the policy did not prove itself to be sufficiently effective. Admittedly the funding operation did lead to a slight reduction in the commercial banks' cash reserves. It is perhaps also true that in 1963 the volume of the commercial banks' other liquid assets did not increase as much as it might have in the absence of the funding operation. But the fact remains that in 1963 the commercial banks managed to expand their loans and advances by no less than 25%. It must, however, be noted that this expansion in the commercial banks' lending to the non-government sector led to a significant fall in their cash and liquidity ratios. As can be seen from table 2, these ratios fell respectively from 15 and 51% in 1962 to 8 and 41% in 1963. That the commercial banks were able to let these ratios drop so drastically is explained by the fact that until April 1964, the banks in Ghana were under no legal obligation to maintain any fixed cash and liquidity ratios and, therefore, kept such voluntary ratios as they found convenient.

It is obvious, then, that government borrowing in 1963 followed a pattern, which normally would have reduced the commercial banks' ability to expand their credit to the rest of the economy, which, however, in the absence of statutory minimum cash and liquidity ratios, failed to exert any retarding influence on the process of monetary expansion. The situation became explosive in the last quarter of 1963 when, following the seasonal pattern of cocoa financing, the demand for bank credit reached its peak with the consequence of plunging down the commercial banks' cash and liquidity ratios to about 6 and 25% respectively [28].

Alarmed by the aggressive lending policy of the commercial banks and their disregard of sound banking practice, the Bank of Ghana introduced a series of credit control regulations. One of the primary aims of these regulations, which came into effect on 1st April, 1964, was to discipline the commercial banks and to regulate the level of their credit. Under the new regulations,

---

27 Cf. *Bank of Ghana Report*, June 1964, pp. 48 and 50. This conversion took place in August, 1963, and is, therefore, not fully brought out by the twelve – monthly average figures given in table 1.
28 *Ibid.*, pp. 76.

the commercial banks were required to cover their total deposit liabilities (i.e., demand, time and savings deposits) by at least 8% cash reserves (i.e., cash in tills, current account balances with the Bank of Ghana and net balances with other banks in Ghana) and to maintain no less than 40% between 1st March and 31st August and 46% between 1st September and 28th February in the form of other liquid assets (i.e., Ghana Government Treasury Bills, approved industrial and agricultural loans, and balances in a special account with the Bank of Ghana). In addition to these statutory minimum assets ratios, the commercial banks were required:

- to maintain a minimum of 5% of their total deposit liabilities in a special deposit account with the Bank of Ghana;
- to invest a minimum of 18% of total deposit liabilities in Ghana Government stocks;
- to cover sight balances due to banks abroad (including head office, correspondents, foreign branches and subsidiaries) by 100% foreign currency deposits with the Bank of Ghana;
- to obtain prior approval of the Bank of Ghana before granting loans exceeding £G5,000 for purposes other than agriculture and industry; and
- to obtain and deposit with the Bank of Ghana a minimum of 15% down payment before opening a letter of credit in respect of imports of consumer goods including consumer durables[29].

The evidence is, however, strong that on the whole these measures were not effective in arresting the growth of bank credit to the non-government sector[30]. As can be seen from table 1, the commercial banks' loans and advances continued to grow apace, reaching an all time peak of £G40.3 million in 1965[31]. The expansion in the bank credit to the non-government

---

29 *Ibid.*, pp. 89–90. For further details, *see*, appendix table X.

30 In view of virtual ineffectiveness of these measures, it became necessary for the Bank of Ghana to introduce further monetary measures. In January 1966 the Bank Rate was increased from 4.5% to 7% and the commercial banks were required to reflect this increase in their lending rates. At the same time, the commercial banks were asked to reduce their lending for relatively less productive purposes by rates ranging from 10 to 50%. In addition, as a further step towards reducing bank lending to the commercial sector, the commercial banks were asked to submit all letters of credit to the Bank of Ghana for approval, and to obtain and deposit with the Bank cash margins of 5% in respect of raw materials and 1% in respect of capital goods. Finally, in March 1966, as a further safeguard against an undue expansion in bank credit, the Bank of Ghana undertook to ensure that commercial banks' credit did not exceed the "ceiling", which was agreed upon between the IMF and the Bank. *Cf. Bank of Ghana Report*, June 1966, pp. 36–37.

31 There was, however, a notable shift in the end-use of the commercial banks' credit in favour of the agricultural sector (including fishing) even though the greatest proportion continued to go to the commercial sector.

sector in 1964 and 1965 was in fact greater than is borne out by the figures of loans and advances. This is because with the introduction of a new method of cocoa financing in the 1963/64 main crop season, the commercial banks' credit for cocoa financing increasingly took the form of rediscounting of internal bills drawn on the Cocoa Marketing Company[32]. As a result, the commercial banks' portfolio of other bills went up from £G2.2 million in 1963 to £G11.3 million in 1965 (table 1)[33]. It is likely that had there been no change in the method of cocoa financing, the commercial banks' loans and advances in 1964 and 1965 would have increased to a much higher level. To obtain a clearer picture of the extent of the commercial banks' lending to the non-government sector in 1964 and 1965 and to make it comparable with that of the previous years, it is therefore reasonable to add the figures of internal cocoa bills discounted by them to those of their loans and advances. When this is done, we find that between 1962 and 1965 the commercial banks' lending to the non-government sector more than doubled.

Note, however, that in table 1 the internal cocoa bills are included under liquid assets. This is explained by the fact that like treasury bills, internal cocoa bills are rediscountable with the Bank of Ghana. This, however, is only a part of the explanation for the expansion in the commercial banks' liquid reserves in 1964 and 1965 as shown by table 1. In part this expansion also resulted from the resumption of the sale of treasury bills to the commercial banks as a means of financing the growing budgetary deficits. The reversion to the pattern of government borrowing established in 1960–62 was inconsistent with the foremost aim of the statutory minimum reserves requirements and other restrictive measures introduced in April 1964, viz. to reduce the commercial banks' ability to expand their credit to the non-government sector. For by increasing its sale of treasury bills to the commercial banks, the Government swelled their liquid reserves and thereby made the money-credit system more elastic. And, under the impetus of growing demand for credit for cocoa financing, the commercial banks on the whole were now even less willing (or able) to hoard liquidity than they were before the introduction of the legal reserves requirements.

---

32 For details of the method of cocoa financing before the 1963/64 main crop season, *see,* appendix B.

33 The significant increase in the commercial banks' holding of cocoa bills in 1965 resulted partly from the bumper cocoa crop in 1964/65 main season and partly from the decision of the Government in October 1964 to hold-up cocoa export. Ghana withdrew from the market together with the other members of the Cocoa Producers' Alliance (Brazil, Cameroon, Ivory Coast, Nigeria and Togo) with the aim of preventing the price of cocoa from falling below the 'indicator' price of £G190 per long ton. Since despite this withdrawal the cocoa price did not show any improvement, in February 1965 the Alliance members decided to resume sales. *Cf.* Bank of Ghana: *Quarterly Economic Bulletin,* Vol. 5, No. 1 (March 1965), p. 5.

A closer look at table 2 confirms the above conclusion on the commercial banks' propensity to lend. Apparently, there was an improvement in the commercial banks' cash ratio in 1964 and 1965. It must, however, be pointed out that the increase in cash ratio was in part due to the inclusion of funds which were due for transfer abroad but in view of foreign exchange difficulties were temporarily held up[34]. Thus, the 'actual' cash ratio in 1964 and 1965 was perhaps not considerably higher than that in 1963 or the legal minimum (8%). Nor should we be misled by the sudden jump in the other liquid reserves ratio from 41% in 1963 to 67% in 1964. For, as indicated earlier, under the legal minimum requirements these assets were defined to include approved industrial and agricultural loans as well[35]. It is also noteworthy that, although collectively the three commercial banks managed to meet the minimum cash and liquidity requirements[36], on the whole they failed to fulfil the other statutory obligations. For, as can be seen from table 2, their special deposits with the Bank of Ghana remained considerably below the minimum of 5%. Similarly, throughout the period they were unable to fulfil the obligation to hold Ghana Government securities equivalent to 18% of their total deposit liabilities[37].

The foregoing analysis suggests the following conclusions. First, during 1960–65 government borrowing from the commercial banks witnessed a significant increase. Second, a large part of this borrowing took the form of treasury bills, which augmented the commercial banks' liquid reserves. In other words, government borrowing from the commercial banks was a source of elasticity in the money-credit system. Third, due to this increase in their credit-creating potential, the commercial banks were able to extend an

---

34 Note, however, that the commercial banks treated such funds as part of their cash reserves, but excluded them from their deposits liabilities. *Cf. Bank of Ghana Report,* June 1966, p. 37.

35 In the absence of the data on the commercial banks' loans for approved industrial and agricultural purposes it is not possible to make the necessary adjustment with a view to make the figures for 1964 and 1965 comparable with those for 1963.

36 One of the commercial banks, the Ghana Commercial Bank, could not, however, fulfil even the minimum cash and liquidity requirements. The persistent inability of the Ghana Commercial Bank can be attributed to the fact that, even though with the introduction of internal cocoa bill system in 1963/64 main crop season the Bank lost its virtual monopoly for cocoa financing, it continued to play a major role in this field with the consequence that more often than not it was over-lent. The Bank's cash and liquidity ratios continued to remain well below the minimum requirements until during the first half of 1966 when, on behalf of the Government, it received from the Bank of Ghana a sum of about £G14 million under the I.M.F. stabilization programme. *Cf. Bank of Ghana Report,* June 1966, p. 36.

37 In fairness to the commercial banks it must, however, be mentioned that this was not always their fault, because at times the supply of Ghana Government stocks was inadequate. *Cf. Bank of Ghana Report,* June 1964, p. 79.

increasing amount of credit to the non-government sector as and when the demand for 'credit-worthy' loans by this sector increased. This means that in Ghana during the period under review government borrowing from the commercial banks was essentially expansionary.

It is evident, then, that the definition of deficit financing relevant to the present study is the second one, viz. the increase in the government net borrowing from the central bank and the commercial banks.

6. Method of Estimation

It is not possible to calculate deficit financing directly from the government budgets because of inadequacy of the published data on government borrowing according to the sources of borrowing. Consequently, it is necessary to use an indirect method of estimation, viz. by analysing the "causative" (compensatory and offsetting) factors of changes in the money supply from the data on the consolidated balance sheets of the banking system published in the Bank of Ghana annual reports. This has been done in table 3 which traces the origin of the changes in the money supply in Ghana during 1960–65. Details of the methods of derivation of various items and the necessary qualifications and limitations of the data are set out in appendix A. Only two or three main points need to be noted here. The money supply in Ghana is defined in the conventional manner to include currency in active circulation and general demand deposits. In recent years, the appropriateness of this definition of money supply has been often questioned, especially for economies with a mature financial system, on the ground that it is based on a somewhat arbitrary distinction between money and quasi-money. It has been for instance argued that since in practice time deposits are quite often used as a substitute for demand deposits, the definition of money supply must be enlarged to include time deposits. We have in this study adhered to the conventional definition of money supply for the reason that, because the commercial banks in Ghana in general insist on an appropriate notice of withdrawal[38], the scope for using time deposits as current account deposits is rather limited. In table 3, the net accruals to time and savings deposits (as well as to mandatory deposits against letters of credit) have, thus, been considered as offsets to the commercial banks' lending to the non-government sector and are subtracted from column 6 to obtain the net contribution of this sector to the money supply. The net effect of the government sector on the money supply, which is defined here as deficit financing, is calculated by subtracting government deposits from the total of government current loans and long-term credit and securities.

---

38 Time deposits are held at fixed terms for periods of three months or more.

Table 3. Deficit Financing, 1960–65
(₤G million)

Year	Increase in Money Supply (4+7+8+9) 1	Government Sector Deficit Financing Increase in Government net borrowing			Increase in Non-Government Sector's net borrowing			Accumulation of Foreign Reserves by the Banking System 8	Increase in Capital and other Accounts of the Banking System 9
		From Bank of Ghana 2	From Commercial Banks 3	Total (2+3) 4	From Bank of Ghana 5	From Commercial Banks[a] 6	Total (5+6) 7		
End of Year									
1960	10.0	0.0	4.2	4.2	0.0	3.2	3.2	6.1	−3.5
1961	5.8	7.8	2.8	10.6	0.0	6.8	6.8	−11.8	0.2
1962	8.6	6.8	7.4	14.2	0.0	−0.7	−0.7	− 2.9	−2.0
1963	4.7	2.9	3.1	6.0	14.5	7.8	22.3	−16.3	−7.3
1964	34.5	12.4	19.3	31.7	18.6	−5.3	13.3	− 5.8	−4.7
1965	−0.6	34.1	−2.0	32.1	−10.8	16.2	5.4	−32.1	−6.0
Average 1960–1965	10.5	10.7	5.8	16.5	3.7	4.7	8.4	−10.5	−3.9
Average of Year									
1960	6.1	0.0	3.8	3.8	0.0	1.4	1.4	n.a.	n.a.
1961	8.8	5.5	3.0	8.5	0.0	8.3	8.3	n.a.	n.a.
1962	4.8	5.8	8.1	13.9	0.0	−1.3	−1.3	n.a.	n.a.
1963	8.4	10.0	4.2	14.2	2.7	3.2	5.9	− 8.6	−3.1 [b]
1964	17.1	−2.3	7.4	5.1	11.5	−2.2	9.3	1.3	1.4 [b]
1965	21.3	20.5	12.5	33.0	11.4	5.4	16.8	−20.4	−8.1 [b]
Average 1960–1965	11.1	6.6	6.5	13.1	4.3	2.5	6.8	n.a.	n.a.

a Net of changes in time, savings and other deposits.
b Calculated as a balancing item.

A further point to note is that table 3 provides data on year-end as well as twelve-monthly average basis[39]. A year-by-year comparison of the data on deficit financing (column 4) given in the two parts of the table reveals considerable differences. Note in particular the strikingly opposite results obtained for 1963 and 1964: while for 1963 the year-end figure is much lower than the monthly-average figure, for 1964 the year-end figure is strikingly higher than the monthly-average figure. Taking the period as a whole, however, there is tolerable agreement between the two sets of figures. As will be argued later on[40], because of strong seasonal trends in bank credit and money supply, the year-end figures give a somewhat exaggerated idea of the monetary situation. Even though our data on certain items for the first three years are not complete, monthly-average figures of money supply and bank lending to the government and non-government sectors are considered to give a better idea of the trends in the period as a whole. In what follows, therefore, we shall base our analysis on the data given in the lower half of the table.

7. Estimates of Deficit Financing

It can be seen from the lower part of table 3 that the rate of deficit financing increased persistently in the first four years from £G3.8 million to £G14.2 million. It fell significantly in 1964 to £G5.1 million, but rose again in 1965 to an all time peak of £G33 million. The perceptible decrease in the rate of deficit financing in 1964 is explained by the fact that between September 1963 and June 1964 the Government took over the foreign assets of certain statutory bodies and public institutions and sold them to the Bank of Ghana, which paid their counter-value into the account of the Government. As compensation for the foreign assets surrendered by them, the statutory bodies and public institutions received Government stocks[41]. This triangular transaction, which is supposed to have totalled between £G40 million and £G50 million, helped the Government a great deal in financing its budgetary deficits and had the effect of reducing its need for borrowing from the banking system. Since the funds so acquired were in excess of the Government's immediate requirements, they were utilized gradually. As a result, the volume of government net borrowing from the banking system in the first half of 1964 did not witness any significant increase over its level during the corresponding period in 1963. It is obvious that but for this transaction

---

39 Because of inadequacy of the published data it has not been possible to calculate twelve-monthly averages for foreign assets and capital and other accounts of the banking system for the first three years of the period under review.
40 Chapter II.
41 So that in 1963 government long-term borrowing from the domestic non-bank sector increased significantly.

the rate of deficit financing in 1963 and 1964 would have been considerably higher[42]. It is also evident that the transaction was a temporary source of financial relief to the Government. For 1965 saw not only a reversion to the earlier pattern but also a significant increase in the Government's reliance on the banking system for financing its growing budgetary deficit.

The average annual rate of deficit financing during 1960–65 was about £G13 million, of which half was contributed by the Bank of Ghana and the other half by the commercial banks. Note, however, that whereas the commercial banks' contribution was fairly evenly distributed in the six-year period that of the Bank of Ghana was concentrated in 1963 and 1965. Consequently, the relative importance of the commercial banks and the Bank of Ghana as sources of deficit financing varied significantly from year to year. As can be seen from table 3, in 1960 the commercial banks were the sole source of deficit financing[43]. This position changed significantly in 1961 when out of the total deficit financing of £G8.5 million, the Bank of Ghana contributed £G5.5 million or about 65%. The commercial banks' contribution rose to 58% in 1962 but fell again to less than one-third in 1963. The year 1964 saw a different pattern of deficit financing. In that year, as a result of the triangular transaction mentioned earlier, there was a reduction in the level of the Government's net indebtedness to the Bank of Ghana[44], whereas, in part as a result of the introduction of statutory minimum liquidity ratio, the amount of Government net borrowing from the commercial banks went up significantly over its level in the previous year. In 1965 the Government increasingly turned to the banking system for financing its budgetary deficit, but as can be seen from table 3, the weight of additional borrowing shifted significantly from the commercial banks to the Bank of Ghana, which contributed about two-thirds of the total deficit financing.

8. Deficit Financing and Budget Deficits

Although our estimates of deficit financing have been arrived at indirectly, they can be broadly related to the size of budget deficits and the level of government capital expenditures. To facilitate this exercise, the available

---

42 The immediate effect of this transaction was to reduce the rate of government net borrowing from the banking system in the last quarter of 1963 with the result that the over-all dose of deficit financing in 1963 was only slightly higher than in 1962.

43 It is noteworthy that before 1960 the commercial banks were a small net debtor to the Government whereas borrowing from the Bank of Ghana was negligible. Hence, deficit financing by the Ghana Government was for the first time resorted to in 1960, when the commercial banks' position *vis-a-vis* the Government changed from a small net debtor to a net creditor.

44 From £G 19.9 million in 1963 to £G17.6 million. *See,* appendix table VII.

data on budget deficits and government capital expenditures have been converted from the fiscal years to the calendar years[45]. Table 4 gives these data for the period 1958–65.

It is evident from the table that the size of budget deficit has been closely related to the rate of government capital expenditure. The continuous deterioration in the budgetary position from a surplus of £G6.1 million in 1958 to a record deficit of £G51.1 million in 1964 resulted largely from a persisent increase in government capital expenditure from £G14.9 million to £G54.1 million over the same period. That despite a further jump in government capital expenditure by £G16.9 million the size of budget deficit in 1965 was considerably smaller than in 1964 is explained by the fact that between the two years the Government was able to increase its current revenue by no less than 39%. Since this spectacular increase in current revenue was not accompanied by a correspondingly high rate of increase in current expenditure, the level of current revenue surplus available for financing government capital expenditure jumped from £G3 million in 1964 to £G32 million in 1965[46].

Table 4. **Capital Expenditure, Budget Deficit and Deficit Financing, 1958—65**

	1958	1959	1960	1961	1962	1963	1964	1965	Average 1960—65
Capital Expenditure (£G million)	14.9	22.1	34.4	43.0	50.3	52.4	54.1	71.0	51
Budget Deficit (£G million)	–6.1	4.4	24.8	37.8	45.8	47.4	51.1	39.0	41
Deficit Financing (£G million)	–	–	3.8	8.5	13.9	14.2	5.1	33.0	13
Deficit Financing as % of Budget Deficit	–	–	15	22	30	30	10	85	32

Sources: Derived from table 3 and appendix table XIV.

Almost one-third of the total budget deficit during 1960–65 was financed through money creation. However, as can be seen from table 4, the relative importance of deficit financing varied considerably from year to year. While

45 During the period under review, the fiscal year in Ghana was changed twice: in 1962 from July/June to October/September and in 1965 from October/September to January/December. The figures for calendar years have been derived from the available data for fiscal years by using half-yearly or quarterly averages. After the coup in February 1966, the fiscal year was once again changed to July/June.
46 For further details, *see,* appendix table XIV.

in 1960 only 15% of the budget deficit was financed through money creation, during 1962–63 the relative significance of deficit financing rose close to one-third. This position changed significantly in 1964 when for the first time during the six-year period under review the ratio of deficit financing to the budget deficit fell to 10%. In sharp contrast, in 1965 deficit financing rose to an alarming proportion. In that year more than four-fifths of the budgetary gap was covered by the creation of money.

The explanation for these wide year-to-year variations in the relative importance of deficit financing is to be found in the nature and the size of the other resources available to the Government. Up till 1961 the growing gap between overall budgetary expenditure and current revenue was covered mostly by drawing down the external reserves. In part the budgetary deficits were also financed by receipts from the voluntary contributions of cocoa farmers to national development, and loans from the Cocoa Marketing Board[47]. Consequently, up to 1961 the need for large scale borrowing from the banking system had not arisen.

Having used up most of its external assets and faced with an even bigger budgetary deficit in 1962, the Government was compelled to step up its internal borrowing from non-inflationary sources and to seek loans from abroad. At the same time, the Government took a number of measures to increase revenue from taxation. Though during 1962–63 there was a significant increase in government receipts both from taxation and other non-inflationary sources, it was by no means adequate to fill-in the budgetary gaps. Increase in government borrowing from the banking system therefore became inevitable.

It may seem surprising that despite a further increase in the size of budgetary gap in 1964, the relative significance of deficit financing in that year was considerably lower than in the earlier years. To be sure, the perceptible decline in the rate of deficit financing in 1964 did not result from any increase

---

47 The system of voluntary contributions from cocoa farmers was introduced in May 1959. The Cocoa Marketing Board was authorized to collect these contributions on behalf of the Government at the fixed rate of £G22/8/- per ton. Government receipts from this source amounted to £G5.6 million in 1959/60 and £G 11 million in 1960/61. However, due to heavy trading losses incurred by the Board in 1961/62 and 1962/63, it could not remit the voluntary contributions to the Government. These arrears, £G8 million in respect of 1961/62 and £G10.6 million for 1962/63, were paid off in 1963/64, when for this purpose the Government repaid the Board a sum of £G18.6 million in respect of the loans obtained previously. The sum so received was then used by the Board to pay off its arrears of voluntary contributions.

It is obvious that these transactions between the Government and the Board were simply an act of "window dressing". In the final analysis, these transactions did not lead to any net increase in the budgetary resources available to the Government during the fiscal year 1963/64.

in current account surplus. For, as can be seen from appendix table XIV, largely due to a further jump in government current expenditure, the level of current savings fell from £G5 million in 1963 to £G3 million in 1964. The decrease in the relative importance of deficit financing in 1964 was against the background of a big jump in government internal borrowing from the non-bank sector as well as the increase in the inflow of foreign capital. While the increase in external borrowing took the form mainly of medium-term suppliers' credit, the issue of Compensatory Stocks (in exchange for foreign securities surrendered by certain statutory bodies and public institutions) was the predominant source of internal borrowing from non-inflationary sources. As indicated earlier, but for this 'compulsory' borrowing from the non-bank sector, both the absolute level and the relative share of deficit financing in 1964 would have been considerably higher.

It is noteworthy that even though the size of budget deficit was significantly smaller in 1965 than in 1964, deficit financing was much higher in the former year than in the latter year. It is also significant that the phenomenal rise in the relative significance of deficit financing in 1965 took place despite the Government's initial intention of keeping its borrowing from the banking system at an extremely low level and notwithstanding the strong recommendation by the IMF-IBRD Mission to limit the overall budgetary expenditure to an amount that could be financed through current revenue and non-inflationary borrowing[48]. The sharp rise both in the absolute level and the relative share of deficit financing in 1965 stemmed from the Government's failure to arrest its mounting expenditure, even though its hope of getting long-term credits from abroad had by and large proved unfounded[49], and the scope for squeezing further internal loans from non-inflationary sources was extremely restricted. The reliance on borrowing from the banking system in 1965 became indeed so inevitable and so heavy that for the first time the statutory limit of Ways and Means Advances[50] from the central bank was

---

48 *Cf. The Budget 1965*, p. 18, and *1965 Supplementary Budget Statement*, pp. 3–4.

49 For further details, *see*, N. AHMAD: "Some Aspects of Budgetary Policy in Ghana", *The Economic Bulletin of Ghana*, Vol. X (1966), No. 1, pp. 3–22.

50 Under the *Bank of Ghana Act, 1963*, the Bank is authorized to make Ways and Means Advances to the Government in respect of temporary deficiencies of budget revenue. The Act stipulates that:
- "the total amount of such advances shall not at any time exceed ten *per centum* of the estimated budget revenue, as laid before the National Assembly, for the financial year in which the advances are made" (p. 18, para. 37 [1]);
- "subject as aforesaid the Bank may in certain cases make advances not exceeding fifteen *per centum* of the estimated budget revenue if the President so requests" (p. 18, para. 37 [2]); and,
- "any advance made under this section shall be repaid within three months of the end of the financial year to which it relates; and if any such advance remains unpaid after that date the power of the Bank to make further

virtually exhausted and the Government had to resort to a special loan of
£G12.5 million from the Bank of Ghana[51].

---

advances in any subsequent financial year shall not be exercisable unless the amounts due in respect of outstanding advances have been repaid" (p. 19, para. 37 [3]).

51 The need for this special loan arose towards the end of 1965, when according to the statutory regulations referred to above, the repayment of a sum of £G20 million in respect of Ways and Means Advances became due. The proceeds from the special loan were used by the Government to meet its outstanding obligation to the Bank of Ghana. In effect, the special loan was yet another device invented by the Government to keep its borrowing from the Bank at a high level without contravening the statutes of the Bank of Ghana. It is also noteworthy that the sum of £G20 million repaid to the Bank of Ghana was immediately funded into 5% stock 1967/68 und 6% Special Stock 1975/80. Since a major part of these stocks was probably taken over by the banking institutions, the exercise perforce led to an increase in the Government's indebtedness to the banking system. Cf. Bank of Ghana Report, June 1966, pp. 23–24.

Chapter II

MONETARY EXPANSION IN GHANA: 1960–65

The purpose of this chapter is to provide an over-all view of the monetary and balance of payments developments in Ghana during the six-year period 1960–65. To this end, data will be presented in the framework of the system of monetary analysis developed by the Organization for European Economic Cooperation[1]. We shall start with a description of the O.E.E.C. system of monetary analysis. With some modifications we shall then apply the analytical model to Ghana in order to examine the extent and nature of monetary expansion and its absorption through the increase in monetary liquidity, domestic production growth, price increases and balance of payments deficits. Next the forces behind internal monetary expansion will be analyzed and the role of government deficit finance operations in generating expansionary impulses in the economy will be examined. This will be followed by an extensive study of the behaviour of monetary ratio and the causes of wide year-to-year fluctuations in the relative importance of monetary liquidity as an offseting factor. Finally, the trends in domestic production and balance of payments will be investigated.

1. A System of Monetary Analysis

The O.E.E.C. system of monetary analysis is based on the following equation of sources and uses of funds, which implies that total monetary financing, i.e., the sum of internal credit monetization, external credit monetization, and relative contraction of monetary liquidity, must be fully absorbed by growth in domestic production, increase in prices and balance of payments deficit:

$$F_i + F_e + F_m = K_o (X - X_o) P_o + K_o (P - P_o) X + D \quad . \quad . \quad . \quad (1)$$

where, on the sources side:

---

1 Organization for European Economic Cooperation, *Statistics of Sources and Uses of Finance, 1948–1958*, Paris, 1960.

47

F_i = internal credit monetization by the domestic banking system, i.e., that portion of the expansion in the domestic banking system's internal assets, or gross lending, of which the counterparts appear either in an increase of the money supply or in a decrease of the banking system's net gold and foreign assets, rather than in an increase of its internal liabilities other than money.

F_i can, thus, be defined:

either, $F_i = \triangle A_{bi} - \triangle L_{bi}$ . . . . (2)

where $\triangle A_{bi}$ and $\triangle L_{bi}$ denote respectively the increase in the banking system's internal assets and the increase in its domestic liabilities other than money;

or, $F_i = \triangle M + \triangle N_b$ . . . . (3)

where $\triangle M$ and $\triangle N_b$ are respectively the increase in the money supply and the decrease in the net gold and foreign assets of the banking system[2].

F_e = external credit monetization, which is defined as the net foreign disinvestment — that is, liquidation of the previously accumulated foreign assets and the net increase in borrowing from abroad — by the non-bank sector of the economy.

F_e is therefore equal to the sum of the net decrease in the non-bank sector's foreign assets, $\triangle N_n$, and the net increase in the sector's external liabilities, $\triangle L_{ne}$:

$F_e = \triangle N_n + \triangle L_{ne}$ . . . . (4)

F_i and F_e as defined above represent respectively the internal and external components of the total injection of new money into the economy. For a correct interpretation of the term monetization and in order to obtain a better idea of the two forms of money creation we can de-consolidate them into:

$F_i = F_{ig} + F_{ip}$ . . . . (5)

$F_e = F_{eg} + F_{ep}$ . . . . (6)

where the subscripts g and p indicate the components of the government sector and the non-government sector respectively. Accordingly, we can define internal credit monetization, F_i, as that part of the money creation which results from the net credits obtained by the government sector, F_{ig}, and the non-government sector, F_{ip}, from the domestic banking system.

---

2 Increase in the domestic banking system's internal assets, or gross bank lending, $\triangle A_{bi}$, can thus be calculated:

either, $\triangle A_{bi} = \triangle M + \triangle N_b + \triangle L_{bi}$ . . . . (3a)

or, $\triangle A_{bi} = \triangle F_i + \triangle L_{bi}$ . . . . (3b)

Similarly, we can define external credit monetization, F_e, as that part of the money creation which has its origin in the net credits obtained by the government sector, F_{eg}, and the non-government sector, F_{ep}, from abroad.

Note, however, that while F_{ip} and F_{ep} immediately lead to a corresponding increase in the money supply, F_{ig} and F_{eg}, strictly speaking, create cash, not money. F_{ig} and F_{eg} assume the character of money only when the cash acquired by the government passes into the non-government sector either through the purchase of goods and services or by lending or by transfers. In other words, while F_{ip} and F_{ep} are monetized directly, in case of F_{ig} and F_{eg} the process of monetization is an indirect one. This formal distinction in the process of monetization notwithstanding, the term credit monetization is used in the present model to denote all those credit transactions which lead to money creation irrespective of whether the process of monetization is direct or indirect.

F_m = relative contraction of monetary liquidity, which is equal to the difference between the cash balances which the public would have held on the basis of the previous year's monetary (money: income) ratio, YK_0, and the cash balances actually held by the public, YK.

Thus, $F_m = Y(K_0 - K)$ . . . . (7)

where Y is the current year's gross national product in current prices, and K_0 and K[3] are respectively the money-income ratios of the preceding year and the current year.

F_m, therefore, represents the 'activation' of money supply through a reduction in the monetary ratio or, in other words, through an increase in the velocity of circulation of money[4]. Accordingly, F_m can also be calculated as the difference between the additional monetary requirements on the basis of the previous year's ratio, $K_0(Y - Y_0)$,[5] and the actual increase in money supply (money holdings), $\triangle M$.

$$F_m = K_0(Y - Y_0) - \triangle M \quad . . . . (8)$$

On the uses side:

$K_0(X - X_0)P_0$ = the increase in monetary requirements connected with the increase in domestic production; $K_0(X - X_0)P_0$ denotes the excess of the current year's national

---

3 In the original version of the equation, monetary ratio is denoted by u. We have, however, adhered to the more common practice of denoting money-income ratio by K.

4 Money-income ratio, K, is the inverse of velocity of circulation of money, V, i.e., $K = 1/V$, or, $V = 1/K$.

5 $K_0(Y - Y_0)$ represents the amount by which the money supply would have increased if people had retained during the current year the same ratio of money to income as they had in the previous year.

production at constant prices, X,[6] over the previous year's national production in real terms, X_0, evaluated at the previous year's prices, P_0, and adjusted for the previous year's monetary ratio, K_0.

$K_0 (P - P_0) X =$ absorption of funds through the increase in internal prices; $K_0 (P - P_0) X$ denotes the increase in price level (GNP deflator) in the current year, P, over the price level in the previous year, P_0, adjusted for the current year's national production at constant prices, X, and for the previous year's monetary ratio, K_0.

$D =$ deficit on current account[7]; D is equal to the decrease in the net gold and foreign assets of the banking system and the non-bank sector, $\triangle N_b$ and $\triangle N_n$, *plus* the increase in the non-bank sector's external liabilities, $\triangle L_{ne}$.

$$D = \triangle N_b + \triangle N_n + \triangle L_{ne} \quad \dots \dots \dots \dots \dots \dots \dots \quad (9)$$

To recapitulate, we may now derive the above monetary equation (1) by using the definitional identities (3), (4), (7) and (8). From (3) and (4) above, we have

$$F_i + F_e = \triangle M + \triangle N_b + \triangle N_n + \triangle L_{ne} \quad \dots \dots \dots \dots \quad (10)$$

by substituting (9) into (10), we get

$$F_i + F_e = \triangle M + D \quad \dots \dots \dots \dots \dots \dots \dots \quad (11)$$

Again, from (7) and (8) above

$$Y (K_0 - K) = K_0 (Y - Y_0) - \triangle M \quad \dots \dots \dots \dots \dots \quad (12)$$

or, $\triangle M = K_0 (Y - Y_0) - Y (K_0 - K) \quad \dots \dots \dots \dots \quad (13)$

---

6 In the original equation, domestic production in current and constant prices are denoted by Y and y respectively. To avoid any possible confusion resulting from the use of the same alphabet, we have found it more appropriate to denote domestic production in constant prices by X.

7 The original model is based on a narrower concept of balance of payments deficit (D) which excludes transfer payments. This has been done mainly to adhere to the customary concept of external deficit used in the O.E.E.C. member countries, i.e., the one which measures excess of imports of goods and services over exports of goods and services. The exclusion of transfer payments from the concept of current account deficit is, however, counterbalanced by using a correspondingly wider definition of external credit monetization, i.e., the one which includes transfers from abroad.

Since, strictly speaking, transfer payments do not represent credit transactions, we have not, contrary to the procedure used in the original equation, treated them as a financing item and therefore excluded them from our estimates of external credit monetization. To match this change on the sources side of the original equation, we have, on the uses side, retained the more widely used concept of the deficit on current account.

We can rewrite $K_0 (Y - Y_0)$ as:

$$K_0 (Y - Y_0) = K_0 (X - X_0) P_0 + K_0 (P - P_0) X \quad \ldots \ldots \quad (14)$$

If we now substitute (14) into (13), we get

$$\triangle M = K_0 (X - X_0) P_0 + K_0 (P - P_0) X - Y (K_0 - K) \quad \ldots \quad (15)$$

By substituting (15) into (11), we obtain

$$F_i + F_e = K_0 (X - X_0) P_0 + K_0 (P - P_0) X - Y (K_0 - K) + D \quad (16)$$

Since we have already defined $Y (K_0 - K) = F_m$, we can therefore rewrite (16) as:

$$F_i + F_e = K_0 (X - X_0) P_0 + K_0 (P - P_0) X - F_m + D \quad \ldots \quad (17)$$

$$\text{or,} \quad F_i + F_e + F_m = K_0 (X - X_0) P_0 + K_0 (P - P_0) X + D \quad \ldots \quad (1)$$

The foregoing derivation of the monetary equation brings out the following three features of this system of monetary analysis. First, the current credit monetization, $F_i + F_e$, i.e., the injection of new money into the economy, is equated to the increase in money supply, $\triangle M$, *plus* the deficit on current account, D. Secondly, the increase in money supply, $\triangle M$, is apportioned between the increase in monetary liquidity, F_m, and the additional monetary requirements, $K_0 (Y - Y_0)$. Thirdly, the latter ingredient of the increase in money supply, $K_0 (Y - Y_0)$, is split further into two components, one connected with the domestic production growth, $K_0 (X - X_0) P_0$, the other connected with the increase in domestic price level, $K_0 (P - P_0) X$.

It may be noted that the monetary equation outlined above is essentially a modified and extended version of the transactions ($PT = MV$) and cash-balance ($M = KP X$) equations. It is like the other two equations a truism. Again, like the two simpler versions the present equation does not show any chain of causation between the various variables, but merely presents a number of data in the framework of a set of identities and depicts definitional relationship between various *ex-post* magnitudes.

Despite these common limitations, the monetary equation presented here seems to have two major analytical advantages over the transactions and cash-balance versions. The first of these stems from the fact that the present monetary equation covers explicitly the external deficit as well as the various means of financing such deficit. In doing so, the present equation, unlike the other two versions, avoids undue emphasis on the changes in money supply; it rather demonstrates that, insofar as an economy can finance its external deficit by either running down its previously accumulated foreign reserves or borrowing abroad, monetary expansion need not lead to a proportionate increase either in the money supply or the domestic price level. Needless to say, this distinguishing feature makes the present equation more appropriate for an analysis of monetary developments in a highly open economy such as Ghana's.

The second analytical advantage is that the various items on the two sides of the equation can be easily de-consolidated into a number of components which, though based on a set of identities, shed additional light on the process of monetary expansion and absorption in an economy.

These analytical advantages notwithstanding, the present equation has a number of limitations. One of these which calls for comment is the element of arbitrariness involved in the use of previous year's monetary ratio, K_0, in determining the year-to-year changes in monetary liquidity as well as the absorption of funds through domestic production growth and price increase. Obviously, slightly different figures would be obtained for these items if the current year's monetary ratio, K, were used. It may, however, be argued that the use of current year's monetary ratio may not be free from an element of arbitrariness either. The ideal solution would be to calculate or assume a 'normal' monetary ratio, K_n, on the basis of the past experience of the country and to use it throughout. This, however, can be done only at the cost of added complexities, especially if the year-to-year changes in monetary ratio exhibit wide variations, which, as we shall see later, has been the case in Ghana.

2. Application to Ghana

The data on monetary developments in Ghana for the period 1960–65 are presented in table 5. The table is based on the more detailed data contained in appendix table VI. The sources, limitations and method of derivation of some of the figures used in the text and appendix tables are discussed in appendices A and B. The computation of some of the items used in text table 5 and appendix table VI calls for further explanatory and qualifying remarks to avoid misrepresentation and misuse.

The first point to note is that the data on internal credit monetization, F_i, and monetary ratio, K, have been calculated by using the monthly-average instead of the year-end figures of money supply. Consequently, for the sake of consistency, the figures for monetary liquidity as well as the data on the absorption of monetary financing by domestic production growth and price increase have also been arrived at by using these 'average' monetary ratios, i.e., the ratios between the averages of month-end figures of money supply and the GNP. Our decision to use the monthly-average instead of year-end figures of money supply is based on the following two considerations. First, as in many other developing countries, the money supply in Ghana is subject to pronounced seasonal fluctuations. It is generally highest in December and during the first two months of the calendar year and lowest either in August or September. This pattern is in tune with the timing of cocoa purchases from the farmers which normally begin towards the end of the third quarter of the calendar year. After December cocoa purchases fall sharply, but as the cocoa farmers continue to spend the cash received for their crops up to the end of August, the currency flows back to the banking system during the first eight months of the calendar year. An idea of the magnitude of these seasonal fluctuations in the money supply can be had from appendix table II which gives the year-end and monthly-average figures. Note in particular the big difference between the two sets of figures for 1965: while at the end of 1965 the money supply fell by £G0.6 million (0.5%) over its level at the end of 1964, on the monthly-average basis the money supply in 1965 increased by £G21.3 million (23%). In view of the large seasonal fluctuations in the level of money supply in Ghana, the monthly-average figures are considered to be a more appropriate index of monetary developments. Secondly, there is an element of conceptual inconsistency in using the year-end figures for money supply to compute money-income ratios in the sense that in doing so we in fact relate a stock magnitude (money) to a flow magnitude (GNP). To eliminate this difference in timing, we have found it more appropriate to measure monetary ratios on the basis of the monthly-average figures for money supply. Thus, the data given in table 7 are 'average' monetary ratios. And, as mentioned earlier, for consistency's sake these 'average' monetary ratios have been used in the estimation of items 4, 6 and 7 of table 5.

The use of 'average' monetary ratios has, however, created certain complexities in the computation of data on internal credit monetization. Note that our data on internal credit monetization as given in text table 5 and appendix table VI have been arrived at by adding the increase in money supply, computed on the basis of the monthly averages, to the decrease in external assets of the banking system, calculated from the end of one to the end of the next year. This difference in the methods of estimation of the two components has obviously introduced an element of incompatibility in our figures for internal credit monetization. It is evident that to be consistent we should have either used the monthly-average figures for foreign assets of the banking system as well, or computed both the components on the basis of the year-end data. Needless to say, the latter approach would have made it necessary to calculate monetary ratios on the basis of the year-end figures of money supply and thus prevented us from operating on the basis of 'average' monetary ratios. The lack of necessary data, on the other hand, has impeded the application of the former solution. To begin with, the month-end figures for the foreign assets of the banking system are not available for the entire period under review. And, even if it were possible to compute monthly-average data for this item for the entire period, their use in the estimation of internal credit monetization would have, for the sake of consistency, made it necessary to introduce monthly-average concept in the definition of external credit monetization and balance of payments deficit as well — a proposition which is not feasible at least at the present stage of statistical development in Ghana.

In view of the considerations and difficulties mentioned above, we have adhered to our method of computing data on internal credit monetization. But it should be stressed that, even though our approach is not ideal, it is by no means fatal to the model; it has, on the contrary, enabled us to keep the equation balanced. This is because the two components of internal credit monetization are matched by conceptually identical items on the uses side of the equation: the money supply component of internal credit monetization tallies with the absorption of funds through the increases in monetary liquidity, domestic production and internal prices all computed on the basis of 'average' monetary ratios; while, the figures of foreign assets of the banking system and external credit monetization add up to external deficit — all estimated on the year-end basis.

Another point which calls for comment is the derivation of the data on gross bank lending, increase in less-liquid assets of the commercial banks and increase in other domestic liabilities of the banking system (item 1, 2a and 2b of appendix table VI). The figures for gross bank lending have been derived from the monthly-average data on bank lending to the government and non-government sectors as shown in appendix tables VII and IX. The increases in less-liquid deposits with the commercial banks (time and saving deposits, etc.) are also based on the monthly-average concept and have been obtained from appendix table IX. Since for a number of reasons, some of which are mentioned in appendix A, it has not been possible to compute monthly-average data on other domestic liabilities of the banking system, this item has been calculated indirectly by subtracting the sum of internal credit monetization and increase in less-liquid deposits from gross banking lending (i.e., in appendix table VI, item 2b = item 1 — item A — item 2a). Thus, figures of increases in the other domestic liabilities of the banking system represent residuals and must be so considered.

Finally, it may be mentioned that we have included IMF loans and repurchases (item 4 in appendix table VI) under external credit monetization. Note, however, that it would not have mattered much if the IMF positions were reflected in the estimates of internal credit monetization. This is because the magnitude of current credit monetization, which is the more significant aggregate for the purpose of our analysis, would have remained the same. We have, however, included IMF positions in external credit monetization in order to keep the distinction between F_i and F_e as straight as possible.

3. Monetary Developments in Ghana, 1960—65

Having explained the necessary qualifications and limitations of our data, we may now proceed to analyse the monetary and balance of payments developments during the period under study. A mere glance at table 5 reveals the wide year-to-year variations in the absolute level and relative significance of various expansionary and absorbing factors. Note for instance the wide differences in the absolute levels and relative shares of internal and external credit monetization from one year to another. Note also the apparent lack of any correlation between the magnitudes of current credit monetization and the behaviour of monetary liquidity in the years 1961, 1962, 1963 and 1964. Finally, the table shows that the six-year period under review was also marked by significant year-to-year variations in domestic production growth, internal price increases and balance of payments deficit. These year-to-year fluctuations, as we shall see later, resulted mainly from frequent and at times fundamental changes in certain exogenous factors including a number of important policy variables.

All the same, in view of the erratic movements in most of the expansionary and absorbing factors, we have found it difficult to establish any consistent long-run behavioural relationship between them. This difficulty, however,

Table 5. **Monetary Developments in Ghana, 1960—65**
(£G million)

Data for Monetary Analysis	1960	1961	1962	1963	1964	1965
1. Internal Credit Monetization (F_i)	0.0	20.6	7.7	24.7	22.9	53.4
2. External Credit Monetization (F_e)	53.2	44.9	24.5	37.2	34.3	55.8
3. Current Credit Monetization ($F_i + F_e$)	53.2	65.5	32.2	61.9	57.2	109.2
4. Relative Contraction of Monetary Liquidity (F_m)	−2.7	−5.3	−0.1	−1.8	−7.2	−4.5
5. Total Monetary Financing (3 + 4)	50.5	60.2	32.1	60.1	50.0	104.7
Absorbed by:						
6. Increase in Domestic Production $[K_0 (X–X_0) P_0]$	3.6	1.7	3.3	1.8	2.1	0.7
7. Increase in Internal Prices $[K_0 (P–P_0) X]$	−0.2	1.8	1.4	4.8	7.8	16.1
8. Deficit on Current Account (D)	38.7	52.7	28.2	45.7	34.7	81.5
9. Errors and Omissions in Balance of Payments	8.4	4.0	−0.8	7.8	5.4	6.4

Source: Derived from appendix table VI.

should not discourage us from drawing some broad conclusions on the short-term trends in monetary and balance of payments developments during the six-year period under study. To this end we have found it useful to divide the entire period under study into the following 3 sub-periods of two years each: (a) 1960–61; (b) 1962–63; and, (c) 1964–65. Note that this division coincides with the distinction we made earlier in this study between the years when development plans were being implemented (1960–61 and 1964–65) and those when no such plan was in operation (1962–63). This, however, is not the only consideration for comparing monetary developments between these sub-periods. A more important reason is the 'cyclical' nature of behaviour of most of the variables. A closer examination of the data given in table 5 reveals that the upward (downward) trend in one year was almost invariably followed by a retarding (accelerating) tendency in the next year. Thus, for example, the level of internal credit monetization rose and fell in alternate years. The behaviour of other variables, external credit monetization, monetary liquidity, domestic production and current account deficit in balance of payments was also marked by similar oscillations with the result that, except for domestic prices which during the last 3 years rose uninterruptedly, the process of increase or decrease was seldom cumulative. It seems appropriate therefore to analyse the data on two-year instead of yearly basis. Indeed as we shall soon see much of the year-to-year fluctuations disappear if periods of two years are taken.

It can be seen from table 5 that while internal credit monetization rose from some £G21 million during 1960–61 to about £G32 million during 1962–63, external credit monetization fell sharply by £G 36.4 million between the periods. Consequently, the share of external credit monetization in the total monetary expansion (i.e., current credit monetization) declined from about four-fifths during 1960–61 to two-thirds during the next two years. Although the big drop in external credit monetization was partly neutralized by an increase in internal monetary expansion, on the whole, the dose of new money injected into the economy was about one-fifth smaller during 1962–63 than during 1960–61.

The significant fall in the total monetary expansion between 1960–61 and 1962–63 was accompanied by an equally significant decline in the rate of increase of monetary ratio (the inverse of velocity of circulation). During 1960–61, the rapid increase in monetary liquidity (a decrease in income velocity) offset about 7% of the current credit monetization. In contrast, in the next two-year period this factor absorbed only 2% of the total monetary expansion.

It is noteworthy that the relative significance of balance of payments deficit as an accommodating factor remained virtually unchanged between the two periods, absorbing some 86% of the total monetary expansion. The remarkable stability in the role of current account deficit as a cushion to monetary expansion between the two periods, however, hides a significant change in the method of financing these deficits: whereas in 1960–61 as much as 90% of the balance of payments deficit (including errors and omissions) was financed by running down foreign reserves, during 1962–63 the same percentage declined to 37%.

That during 1960–61 there was no serious imbalance between money demand and available supply of goods is evident from the fact that the increase in domestic prices during this period accounted for about one per cent of the total credit monetization. In fact, as we shall see later, owing to an appreciable increase in the availability of local foodstuffs in 1960, the general price index (GNP deflator) in that year fell slightly below its level in 1959. The rate of increase in domestic production, however, slowed down in 1961 and the domestic price level resumed its upward trend. On the whole, in 1960–61, the increase in domestic production offset about 4.5% of the total credit monetization. During the next two years, 1962–63, this figure went up to 5.4%. None the less, despite the growth of domestic production and in spite of a much smaller dose of monetary injection than in the preceding two years, prices rose significantly during 1962–63, accounting for some 7% of the total monetary expansion.

It is evident, then, that between 1960–61 and 1962–63 the relationship between money demand and available goods deteriorated and the inflationary pressures assumed considerable proportions. It is also clear from the above analysis that an important element in these developments was the marked divergence in the behaviour of monetary liquidity betwen the two periods: whereas during 1960–61 the sharp increase in monetary liquidity — that is, the decrease in income velocity of money — was a key factor in mitigating the inflationary impact of credit creation, in 1962–63 prices rose sharply largely because the net increase in monetary liquidity was small and absorbed, on the whole, only a minute portion of the total credit monetization.

The decline in the absolute level of current credit monetization during 1962–63 did not, however, prove to be lasting. During the next two-year period, 1964–65, total credit monetization went up to some £G166 million, i.e., by 40% over its level in 1960–61 and by 77% over that in 1962–63. The principal source of this increase was internal credit monetization which now rose to little over £G76 million. Thus, internal credit monetization during 1964–65 was approximately four times as high as in 1960–61 and almost two-and-one-half times its level in 1962—63. As against this, external credit monetization at £G90.1 million during 1964–65 was 8% lower than in 1960–61 but 50% higher than in 1962–63. The expansionary impact of this huge dose of monetary injection during 1964–65 was, however, somewhat dampened by a sharp upward trend in the rate of increase of monetary ratio.

This latter development restored the relative share of monetary liquidity as an offsetting factor to its 1960–61 level, viz. 7%. All the same, partly owing to a sluggish trend in domestic production and partly due to a marked decrease in the relative importance of balance of payments deficit as an accommodating factor, monetary expansion during 1964–65 aggravated the imbalance between money demand and goods availabilities and thus intensified the inflationary pressures. About 14% of the entire monetary expansion during 1964–65 was absorbed by the increase in prices, while the domestic production growth and the balance of payments deficit offset 1.7% and 77% respectively.

It must be pointed out that domestic production showed this disappointing behaviour during what were the first two years of the *Seven-Year Development Plan*. That in 1965 domestic production had become virtually stagnant is evident from the fact that in that year barely 0.6% of the entire credit monetization was absorbed by this factor. It is also significant to note that the decline in the relative share of balance of payments deficit as an accommodating factor (from 86% during 1962–63 to 77% during 1964–65) did not result from a fall in its absolute level. On the contrary, the absolute level of balance of payments deficit (including errors and omissions) went up to £G128 million during 1964–65 as against £G81 million in 1962–63. In fact, the balance of payments deficit at almost £G88 million in 1965 was the highest ever during the six-year period under review. The fact that even though the absolute level of external deficit was appreciably higher during 1964–65 than during 1962–63, it was in the last two years, rather than in the first two years, that inflationary pressures really gained momentum should not, however, mislead us. The crucial point to note is that surplus imports in 1964–65 did not provide as much leeway for non-inflationary internal monetary expansion as they did in the preceding two years.

In summary, leaving aside the annual fluctuations, the level of total credit monetization increased from £G53.2 million in 1960 to £G109.2 million in 1965 or by little over 100%. At the same time, the composition of total credit creation changed significantly. While internal credit monetization increased from nil in 1960 to about £G53 million in 1965, during the same period external credit monetization rose from some £G53 million to £G56 million. Thus, during the period under study the contribution of internal monetary expansion to the total money creation increased from zero to about one-half. It is also significant to note that, whereas during 1960–61 external credit monetization took the form largely of liquidation of accumulated foreign reserves, in the course of the next four years borrowing from abroad became the major source of external credit monetization. Monetary ratio increased continuously to cushion the impact of monetary expansion, but the annual rate of increase varied between wide limits. The relative significance of monetary liquidity as an offseting factor fell considerably between 1960–61 and 1962–63, but rose again to its 1960–61 level during 1964–65. Between 1960–61 and 1962–63, the relative positions of domestic production growth and balance of payments deficit as offsetting factors remained virtually unchanged. In contrast, during 1964–65, domestic production became increasingly stagnant and, despite a significant increase in its absolute level, the balance of payments deficit assimilated a much smaller proportion of the total monetary expansion than in the preceding two years. The average annual rate of increase in the money supply fell appreciably from 14.5% in 1960–61 to about 10% in 1962–63. Yet, owing to a considerable drop in the rate of expansion in monetary liquidity between the two periods, prices rose more sharply during 1962–63 than during the previous two-year period. On the other hand, during 1964–65, the money supply increased at a rate more than twice as fast as in the previous two-year period and, despite a significant rise in monetary liquidity, the gap between money demand and goods availabilities widened, resulting in mounting inflationary pressures.

4. Internal Credit Monetization

The causes of internal credit monetization in Ghana can best be examined by analysing the trends in bank credit to the government and non-government sectors. To this end, the breakdown of gross bank lending (i.e., without subtraction of increases in less-liquid deposits) by the government and non-government sectors is presented in the following table.

The table below shows that the relative contributions of the government and non-government sectors to the total credit expansion varied widely from year to year. In three years, 1960, 1963 and 1965, the expansion in government credit was more than half of the gross bank lending. In 1962, the

Table 6. **Gross Bank Lending, 1960—65**
(Averages of End-of-Month Figures)
(£G million)

Year	To Government Sector	To Non-Government Sector	Total
1960	3.8	3.2	7.0
1961	8.5	10.5	19.0
1962	13.9	0.9	14.8
1963	14.2	10.3	24.5
1964	5.1	17.0	22.1
1965	33.0	25.2	58.2

Sources: Appendix tables VII and IX.

increase in government borrowing accounted for as much as 94% of the total internal credit creation. In contrast, in 1964 bank lending to the government sector expanded by less than one-fourth of the total credit increase. Despite these significant year-to-year variations in its role in increasing the volume of credit in the economy, the increase in government net borrowing from the banking system, which we have defined as deficit financing in this study, was on the whole a more important force behind monetary expansion than the expansion in bank credit to the non-government sector. During 1960–65, out of £G146 million increase in total bank credit, the government sector claimed about £G79 million, or nearly 55%.

It is also clear from the above table that during the period under review there was no direct and precise relationship between the level of deficit financing by the Government and the expansion in bank credit to the non-government sector. In 1962, for example, bank credit to the non-government sector increased by less than £G1 million, whereas the level of deficit financing rose to almost £G14 million (second largest rise during the six-year period under review). At the other extreme, in 1964 bank credit to the non-government sector increased by £G17 million (second largest rise during the six-year period under review) even though the dose of deficit financing at £G5.1 million was relatively modest (second smallest during 1960–65). This tenuous relationship between the two magnitudes confirms the widely-held view that even though government deficit finance operations tend to increase the capacity of the banking system to create additional credit, there is no *a priori* reason to expect that the volume of bank credit to the non-government sector will increase (or decrease) *pari passu* with an increase (or decrease) in the level of government net borrowing from the banking system.

It seems that the significant decline in the rate of expansion in bank credit to the non-government sector in 1962 and the rapid rise thereafter emanated mainly from the fluctuations in the level of commercial activity, which in Ghana has always been centred on foreign trade. The significant increase in bank lending to the non-government sector in 1960 and 1961 was attributable to the flourishing commercial activity; there was hardly any restriction on imports and under the impetus of growing consumer demand the level of imports rose rapidly, resulting in an increase in demand for bank credit. The extremely modest increase in non-government credit in 1962 reflected the sharp decline in the volume of imports following the replacement of Open General Licence by specific licensing system on 1st December, 1961. In 1963, bank credit to the non-government sector increased sharply, partly because commercial activity picked up again in the wake of a rise in imports, and partly due to the increased involvement of the commercial banks in cocoa financing as a result of the introduction of internal cocoa bill scheme. The significant expansion in non-government credit in 1964 and 1965 was traceable largely to the growing demand for funds by the Cocoa Marketing Board to finance the marketing of the record cocoa crop in the 1964/65 season.

The above analysis brings out two important points. First, the demand for credit was the main determinant of the level of bank lending to the non-government sector. Second, the demand for credit in the non-government sector depended largely upon the level of imports and cocoa finance. Deficit financing by the Government appears to have had at best an indirect effect upon the amount of bank lending to the non-government sector; it tended to increase (or decrease) the level of bank credit to the non-government sector only insofar as it induced (or retarded) commercial, agricultural, industrial and constructional activities in the private sector of the economy.

It is also noteworthy that, whereas during 1960–62 the commercial banks were the sole source of credit to the non-government sector, during 1963–65 the Bank of Ghana became an increasingly important lender to the non-government sector. Bank of Ghana credit to the non-government sector rose from £G 2.7 million in 1963 to £G14.2 million in 1964 and £G25.6 million in 1965 (appendix table IX). The relative significance of the Bank of Ghana as a supplier of credit to the non-government sector increased from less than 8⁰/₀ in 1963 to 27⁰/₀ in 1964 and 33⁰/₀ in 1965. This notable change in the source of credit to the non-government sector was attributable to two factors: first, the increased burden of cocoa financing on the Bank of Ghana, resulting from the introduction of inland cocoa bill scheme introduced in October 1963 and, second, the involvement of the Bank in financing current operations of certain state enterprises. A glance at the breakdown of Bank of Ghana credit to the non-government sector reveals that the first factor was of major importance (appendix A). Because the increase in non-government credit from the Bank of Ghana was largely due to cocoa financing, it is essential to contrast the methods of cocoa financing before and after October 1963 with a view to discover the effects of inland cocoa bill scheme on the Bank of Ghana's credit operations.

During the 1961/62 and 1962/63 cocoa seasons, the Bank's role in cocoa financing was essentially restricted to the conversion of the foreign securities surrendered by the Cocoa Marketing Board into local currency and the transmission of these funds to the Board through the agency of the Ghana Commercial Bank[8]. The foreign securities so obtained were used by the Issue Department of the Bank of Ghana as currency cover. Thus, under this scheme the increase in local currency for cocoa financing was directly linked to and, as required by the 1957 Bank of Ghana Ordinance, fully backed by the

---

8 For further details of this system, and the method of cocoa financing before October 1961, see, appendix B.

accumulation of foreign assets by the Bank[9]. And because under the 1957 Ordinance the assets of the Issue Department were to be kept distinct from those of the Banking Department, the Bank's contribution to cocoa finance was not reflected in the credit operations of the Banking Department.

The replacement of this system of cocoa financing by the inland cocoa bill scheme in October 1963 was against the background of a rising demand for funds to finance the expanding cocoa crops and the increasing inability of the Cocoa Marketing Board to surrender sufficient foreign reserves in lieu of local currency, partly because the downward trend in world cocoa price reduced its current foreign exchange receipts and partly due to the fact that a significant part of its accumulated foreign reserves was locked up in loans to the Government. As a first step towards the new scheme for cocoa financing, in May 1963 the 1957 Ordinance was replaced by a new central banking law, the Bank of Ghana Act, 1963. Then, in September 1963 the foreign assets of all the official institutions including the Cocoa Marketing Board were centralized with the Bank of Ghana. Three important features of the new Act were: first, the removal of strict separation between the Issue Department and the Banking Department[10]; second, the redefinition of currency cover to include Ghana Government Treasury Bills and securities, commercial bills of exchange, and certain categories of securities of governments other than the Government of Ghana; and, third, the provision for a fiduciary issue of up to 40% of currency in circulation, which at the discretion of the Minister of Finance could be raised to a maximum of 60%[11].

---

9 The Ordinance had empowered the Bank to create fiduciary issue up to a maximum of £G12 million. None the less, until April 1961, the Bank continued to back its currency liabilities by 100% sterling. In April 1961, the Bank created the first fiduciary issue by using Ghana Government Treasury Bills. Two months later, the second fiduciary issue was created by the use of Ghana Government stocks.

10 So that since October, 1963, the Bank's contribution to cocoa finance (i.e., the Bank's holding of inland cocoa bills) is reflected in its credit to the non-government sector.

11 Cf. Bank of Ghana Act, 1963, section 15, p. 11. In February, 1967, the Act was amended through a decree by the N.L.C. permitting the Bank, retroactively from 1st July, 1965, to hold Ghana Government Treasury Bills and securities, commercial bills of exchange and promissory notes up to a maximum of 75% of the currency in circulation. The same decree empowered the member of the N.L.C. in charge of Finance to suspend this ceiling.

The fact that the upper limit on fiduciary issue was raised ex post facto from first of July, 1965, suggests that it was only after this date that the Bank of Ghana overstepped the previous maximum permissible limit of 60%. A closer look at the data on currency cover assets and currency in circulation, however, reveals that already in June 1965 the ratio of government securities and other bills held as currency cover to currency in circulation had risen to about 72%. There are two possible explanations for this. One is that the published data on currency cover assets is inaccurate. The other possible explanation is that the Bank of Ghana fulfils the fiduciary issue requirements on quarterly or half-

Under the new scheme of cocoa financing introduced in October 1963 the Cocoa Marketing Board was authorized to draw three-months internal bills on its subsidiary marketing company — the Cocoa Marketing Company, which since October 1961 is domiciled in Accra. On their acceptance by the drawee, these bills were initially to be discounted by the commercial banks. At a later stage, the commercial banks could rediscount the bills with the Bank of Ghana. At end of the original term of 90 days, the bills could be renewed once only for a further period of 90 days[12].

Two features of the inland cocoa bill scheme stand out. The first is that it absolves the Cocoa Marketing Board from the obligation of prior provision of foreign exchange in lieu of local currency. The Board can now finance its purchase of cocoa from domestic producers by borrowing from the banking system on the collateral of the very commodity it buys — that is, technically, against its future foreign exchange receipts, rather than by drawing upon its current foreign exchange balances. This 'advance' financing of the Board's buying operations by the banking system is made possible by the second feature of the scheme which is that it adds an important new element of flexibility to the monetary system. The hitherto more or less automatic link between the supply of currency and the availability of foreign assets is broken by the interjection of inland cocoa bills which, together with Ghana Government Treasury Bill and stock, etc., can be used by the Bank of Ghana to create fiduciary issue. Moreover, because under the scheme inland cocoa bills are rediscountable with the Bank of Ghana, the acquisition of these local earning assets by the commercial banks increases the scope for credit creation on a multiple basis.

It must, however, be noted that, although the inland cocoa bill scheme enhances the scope for bank credit to the Board, in principle it need not lead to a continuous increase in the Board's indebtedness to the banking system. This is because credits granted by the banking system against inland cocoa bills are essentially short-term loans which normally would be fully repaid when the Board receives proceeds from export of cocoa. In other words, under normal circumstances, an accelerated expansion in bank credit to the Board in the early phase of cocoa season would be progressively neutralized in the subsequent period.

Yet, in effect, the introduction of inland cocoa bill scheme was followed by a continuous increase in bank lending to the Cocoa Marketing Board. Two factors were responsible for this development. The first was that due to falling world cocoa price and a fixed domestic producer price, the Board's

---

yearly basis, rather than on a monthly basis. *Cf. Bank of Ghana Report*, June 1966, tables 2 and 3, pp. 46–47; and, *Bank of Ghana Report*, June 1967, table 2, pp. 36–37.

12 *Bank of Ghana Report*, June 1963, p. 6.

receipts from cocoa export persistently fell short of its payments to the cocoa farmers with the result that the Board found it increasingly difficult to repay funds borrowed from the banking system. The second factor with the same effect was the hold-up of the bumper cocoa crop in 1964/65 season. During the period of hold-up (from October 1964 to January 1965) the volume of inland cocoa bills held by the banking system went up to a record level. And, because the lifting of ban on sales (on 1st February, 1965) sparked off a further decline in the world cocoa price, the resumption of cocoa export did not provide the Board with sufficient funds to pay off its outstanding debt to the banking system.

The combined effect of all these developments was that cocoa finance became an important force behind monetary expansion. In the 1963/64, 1964/65 and 1965/66 seasons, the cocoa crops were financed mainly by internal bills. In the first instance, these bills were discounted by the commercial banks. Later on, a major portion was rediscounted by the Bank of Ghana. That the burden of cocoa finance fell increasingly on the Bank of Ghana is evident from the fact that out of the total internal cocoa bills of £G17 million outstanding at the end of 1963, the Bank held as much as £G14.5 million or 85.3%[13]. By the end of 1964 inland cocoa bills held by the banking system increased to £G36 million, of which the Bank of Ghana holding amounted to £G32 million or about 90%[14]. As compared to this, at the end of 1965 the Bank of Ghana holding of inland cocoa bills declined to £G20 million due to a fall in the demand for credit for cocoa finance as a result partly of the reduction in domestic producer price in September 1965 and partly of the smaller crop in the 1965/66 season[15].

5. Increase in Less-Liquid Deposits

A continuous increase in less-liquid (time, savings, etc.) deposits with the commercial banks has been an important facet of the monetary developments in Ghana during 1960–65. In accordance with the traditional concept of money supply which is being used in this study, these deposits are treated as non-monetary liabilities of the banking system. Consequently, an increase in these deposits is regarded as a leakage to the process of credit monetization, i.e., credit demonetization.

---

13 *Bank of Ghana Report,* June 1964, p. 66. The lack of data has prevented us from calculating the Bank's holding of internal cocoa bills on monthly-average basis.

14 *Bank of Ghana Report,* June 1965, p. 73.

15 Total outstanding credit for cocoa finance by the banking system amounted to £G43.8 million at the end of 1965, compared with £G50.1 million at the end of 1964. *Cf. Economic Survey,* 1965, pp. 46–47.

The total volume of less-liquid deposits increased uninterruptedly from £G9.7 million in 1959 to £G36.4 million in 1965 (appendix table IX). The increase in these deposits absorbed 18% of the total gross credit creation during 1960–65 (appendix table IX). The ratio of less-liquid deposits with the commercial banks to money supply increased from 20% in 1959 to 32% in 1965 [16]. During the same period, the ratio of less-liquid deposits to demand deposits with the commercial banks rose from 48% to 65% [17].

The increase in the volume of less-liquid deposits in 1964 and 1965 was in part due to the fact that from April 1964 onwards the importers were required to open letters of credit against all imports and to pay in advance a minimum of 15% against these letters of credits. However, even if the expansionary effect of these statutory deposits is excluded [18], the fact remains that between 1963 and 1965 the volume of "voluntary" less-liquid deposits (i.e., time and saving deposits) rose from £G19.5 million to £G29.6 million. Thus, despite the drop in the value of money, accumulation of less-liquid deposits remained an important offset to the total credit creation.

6. Rise in Monetary Ratio

A continuous rise in the monetary ratio has been an important feature of monetary developments in Ghana during the six-year period under review. This phenomenon, though by no means peculiar to Ghana, calls for further comment. As can be seen from table 7, the monetary ratio in Ghana rose from about 0.11 in 1959 to 0.14 in 1965. The overall increase in the monetary ratio over the six-year period works out at 33.5%, i.e., monetary requirements for each unit of output were in 1965 about one-third higher than in 1959. Table 7 also shows that the rate of increase of monetary ratio varied considerably from year to year, ranging from 9% in 1961 to less than 0.3% in 1962. Thus, two features of the behaviour of monetary ratio in Ghana stand out: first, a significant rise over the six-year period, and, second, wide differences in the annual rates of increase. In what follows an attempt will be made to analyse the causes for the secular increase and short-term changes in the monetary ratio in Ghana.

16 Ratio of less-liquid deposits to money supply (in %):

1959	1960	1961	1962	1963	1964	1965
20	21	22	24	27	30	32

17 Ratio of less-liquid deposits to demand deposits (in %):

1959	1960	1961	1962	1963	1964	1965
48	50	51	56	56	63	65

18 These statutory deposits are included under "other accounts". This component of less-liquid deposits increased from £G0.8 million in 1963 to £G3.9 million in 1964 and to £G6.7 million in 1965.

Table 7. **Monetary Ratio, 1959—65**

Year	GNP in Current Prices (Y) (£G million)	Money Supply [a] (M) (£G million)	Monetary Ratio $(K = \frac{M}{Y})$	Increase in Monetary Ratio over previous year $(\triangle K)$	Rate of increase of monetary Ratio $\left(\frac{\triangle K}{K_0} \times 100 \right)$
1959	442	47.47	0.1074	—	—
1960	473	53.56	0.1132	0.0058	5.40
1961	504	62.31	0.1236	0.0104	9.18
1962	542	67.14	0.1239	0.0003	0.24
1963	595	75.54	0.1270	0.0031	2.50
1964	673	92.65	0.1377	0.0107	8.42
1965	795	113.97	0.1434	0.0057	4.13

[a] Average of end of month figures.

We shall begin our analysis by considering those factors which tend to increase monetary ratio in the long run. A secular rise in money-income ratio is generally attributed to the following structural changes which an economy is likely to undergo in the early stages of development:

- a decrease in the relative importance of the non-monetized sector;
- an increase in demand for working balances, i.e., a decrease in income velocity of money held for transactions purposes; and,
- net addition to money hoards.

In a developing economy, the relative importance of the non-monetized sector declines over time, partly because under the influence of wage and price incentives the existing non-monetized sector is gradually monetized and partly because the monetized sector, which includes the dynamic sector of industry, grows more rapidly than the non-monetized rural sector. One important implication of this increase in the significance of monetized sector *vis-a-vis* non-monetized sector is that money is required to perform an additional task of financing transactions which were previously taking place without its mediation. Owing to this gradual expansion in the sphere of influence of money, its stock in a developing economy has to grow at a rate faster than the rise of national income. Consequently, money-income ratio in a developing economy usually shows a marked secular upward trend.

It is safe to assume that, as elsewhere, the process of economic development in Ghana has led to a gradual decrease in the absolute size as well as the relative share of the non-monetized sector. Though precise estimates of the changes in the relative shares of the monetized and non-monetized sectors in the Ghanaian economy are non-existent, a rough idea of the impact which this structural change might have had on the money supply, and hence on the monetary ratio, can be obtained from the following example. Assume that at the beginning of 1960 the non-monetized sector in Ghana stood at one-fourth of the GNP and that by the end of 1965 its share declined to one-fifth. If we further assume that during the six-year period 1960–65, real output did not grow at all and that money-income ratio in the monetized sector remained constant, then given a monetary ratio of 0.1 — more or less the level in 1959 — the money supply in 1965 had to be 6.6% higher than in 1959. This in turn means that by the end of 1965 the monetary ratio should have increased to 0.1066. In other words, on the assumptions outlined above, a decline in the relative share of the non-monetized sector by 5% would in itself lead to an increase in the monetary ratio by 6.6% without causing any inflationary pressures.

There has been in the past quite a controversy over the factors which determine the size of working balances in an economy. Important and fascinating as the controversy has been, it is not necessary for us to enter into its details. Suffice it to say that the notion of an increase in the demand for working balances in a growing economy is based essentially on the argument that in the course of economic development the time-shape of money holdings for transaction purposes undergoes certain changes which in turn cause a downward trend in the income velocity of money. Fundamental to this proposition is the dichotomy between the income-payment and income-expenditure periods discovered by ANGELL who has shown [19] that the demand for working (cash) balances in an economy depends on the degree of 'over-lapping' of the two periods. The income-payment period is defined as the length of time between *like* payments, i.e., from a given 'stage' in production to the next succeeding one, of regularly recurring nature. The income-expenditure period, on the other hand, refers to the length of time a balance is held. The relation between these two magnitudes is called the degree of 'over-lapping'. It is obvious that the extensions of the income-payment and income-expenditure periods would, by lengthening the time required by an average consumer-producer circuit, decrease the income velocity of circu-lation of transactions money, i.e., increase the monetary requirements per unit of output. However, according to ANGELL the main factor which determines the size of working balances in an economy is not the absolute length of income-payment and income-expenditure periods but the degree of their coincidence. He asserts that the demand for working balances would be minimum when the degree of overlapping between the two periods is most efficient or perfect, and maximum when the degree of overlapping is least efficient.

---

19 J. W. ANGELL: "The Components of the Circular Velocity of Money", *The Quarterly Journal of Economics*, Vol. 51 (February 1937), pp. 224–273.

In an attempt to refine ANGELL's exposition, ELLIS has translated the concept of overlapping into the following equation[20]:

$$g = \frac{vL - iL}{vL - m} \quad \ldots \ldots \ldots \ldots \ldots \ldots \ldots \ldots \ldots \quad (1)$$

where, g = the degree of overlapping;
  v = the average income-payment period;
  L = the number of stages in production process;
  i = the average income-expenditure period; and,
  m = the longest income-payment period.

Accordingly, the degree of overlapping will be most efficient (g = 1) when the longest income-payment period (m) encompasses all the income-expenditure periods (iL). At the other extreme, the degree of overlapping will be least efficient (g = o) when the average income-payment period (v) encompasses the average income-expenditure period (i). This means that the monetary requirement will be minimum, i.e., the income velocity of circulation of transactions money will be maximum, when

$$m = iL \quad \ldots \ldots \ldots \ldots \ldots \ldots \ldots \ldots \ldots \ldots \quad (2)$$

On the other hand, the monetary requirement will be maximum, i.e., the income velocity of circulation of transactions money will be minimum, when

$$v = i \quad \ldots \ldots \ldots \ldots \ldots \ldots \ldots \ldots \ldots \ldots \quad (3)$$

Between these two limiting cases of conceivable minimum (g = 1) and maximum (g = o) demand for working balances lie the intermediate cases of monetary requirement (g <1 but >0). Monetary requirement will decrease as the value of g gets closer to one and increase as the value of g approaches zero.

We may now apply the above analysis to the case of Ghana. There are strong reasons to believe that during the six-year period under review the economy of Ghana witnessed significant structural changes in the methods of production, business organization and practices, buying habits and pattern of consumption, etc., resulting in an extension of both the income-payment and income-expenditure periods. The income-payment period can be considered to have increased with the substitution of monthly salaries for weekly wages, of weekly wages for daily wages, as well as with the increase in the number of stages in domestic production (resulting from industrialization). Likewise, it can be argued that the income-expenditure period stretched itself as the emphasis in consumers' behaviour shifted from daily purchases of small units to weekly shopping of relatively large quantities, from basic necessities to

---

20 H. S. ELLIS: "Some Fundamentals in the Theory of Velocity", *Readings in Monetary Theory*, American Economic Association, 1952, pp. 89–128.

consumer durables, from cash payments to payments by cheques and to buying on credit, from spending for immediate consumption to (hopefully) saving for future consumption. Although it is difficult to estimate by how much the two periods increased, it would be safe to assume that the income-payment period tended to increase more rapidly than the income-expenditure period. One important reason for this assumption is the well-known fact that in a traditional society it takes much longer to change consumers' attitude and spending habits than to substitute monthly or weekly wage system for daily wages. It seems, for instance, that although in Ghana most of the workers employed by the Government, state enterprises and big private firms receive their wages on weekly or monthly basis, many of them have stuck to the habit of buying small units of basic necessities for daily consumption largely by paying cash. Viewed in this light, it appears that the structural changes in Ghana have tended to raise m and v more rapidly than i with the result that despite a simultaneous increase in the income-payment and income-expenditure periods, the degree of their overlapping became more imperfect, i.e., g moved closer to zero. The conclusion emerging from this analysis is that the structural changes in Ghana during 1960–65 led to an increase in the demand for working balances so that the money supply in the economy had to increase at a faster rate than the money national income.

A multiplicity of economic and social factors seem to encourage hoarding activity in a country like Ghana. A cocoa farmer, for example, might hoard a part of his receipts as a safeguard against failure of the next crop. A farm worker might decide to keep his savings in the form of idle cash either because of the absence of banking facilities in the rural areas or because of the cumbersome procedure for opening and operating a savings account or simply due to his mistrust of financial institutions. In the urban areas, on the other hand, savings of factory workers and low-grade civil servants may not always find their way to the banking system because of the fear that relatives, tribal 'brothers' and friends might easily come to know about these funds and ask for financial assistance. In case of petty traders, tax evasion might be the main motive for holding savings in the form of notes and coins. Whatever the motive, it is clear that this mode of saving leads to a withdrawal of currency from active circulation and hence to a decline in money demand. To keep the income-expenditure flow unabated, it is therefore necessary in a developing country to offset hoarding function by a regular injection of additional purchasing power. This means that the money supply in a developing economy has to grow more rapidly than the increase in output may warrant, resulting in a continuous increase in the monetary ratio.

One important implication of the above argument is that, like the other structural changes mentioned earlier, hoarding function in a developing country creates a leeway for the 'safe' use of deficit financing[21]. This may at first sight appear to be a valid contention. A closer examination, however, raises serious doubts about the scope provided by hoarding activity for non-inflationary money creation. In the first place, the above argument is based on the assumption that money hoards in a developing country have a secular tendency to grow more rapidly than national income. This in turn implies that (a) in a developing country there is a continuous redistribution of income and wealth in favour of those who prefer to hold their savings in the form of money hoards, and (b) the marginal propensity to hoard either remains constant or increases with increase in income. Although the lack of reliable information prevents us from drawing any precise conclusions on the relevance of these assumptions to the Ghanaian economy, there are reasons to believe that during the period under review the over-all change in the income redistribution, if any, has been against the rural sector. It is doubtful therefore whether, apart from short periods of intensive hoarding due to certain economic or political reasons, net increase in money hoards at a rate faster than the rate of production growth has been a regular feature of the Ghanaian economy. Secondly, it must be realized that since the ultimate objective of keeping unspent incomes in the form of money hoards is to acquire real resources at some future date, the deflationary offset provided by hoarding function is usually a temporary phenomenon. In fact, hoarding function can easily reverse itself and is therefore potentially inflationary. For example, if prices rise continuously and all of a sudden people become inflation-conscious, there may be a strong tendency towards exchanging idle cash balances for goods with the result that the inflationary pressures may be intensified.

---

21 The notion of 'safe' use of deficit financing is essentially based on the argument that insofar as the structural changes mentioned above tend to raise the demand for additional money, they provide scope for non-inflationary money creation by the government for financing capital formation. Accordingly, the price level will remain constant so long as the percentage increase in the money supply ($\triangle M/M$) ist exactly equal to the percentage increase in the output ($\triangle X/X$) plus the percentage increase in the monetary ratio ($\triangle K/K$):

$$\frac{\triangle M}{M} = \frac{\triangle X}{X} + \frac{\triangle K}{K}$$

Thus, for example, if the output grows at an annual rate of 2% and due to the structural changes monetary ratio rises by 4% annually, then a 6% per annum increase in the money supply will be non-inflationary. If we further assume that an increase in government borrowing from the banking system by £G1 would ultimately lead to an increase in the money supply by £G2 then the 'safe' limit of annual deficit financing by the government would be 3% of the money supply.

7. Short-term Behaviour of Monetary Ratio and Price Level: Policy Factors

We may now turn to an analysis of the significant short-term variations in the rate of increase of the monetary ratio. It appears that the sharp rise in the monetary ratio in 1960 and 1961, its virtual stagnation in 1962 and further increases thereafter were at least in part in response to the changes in the Government's policies on wages and incomes, taxation, prices, imports and balance of payments.

Following the introduction of the national minimum wage legislation in July 1960 [22], considerable wage and salary increases were granted to the government employees earning up to £G610 per annum. This action immediately led to similar increases in wages and salaries in the private sector. Gradually middle-ranking civil servants and private employees were also awarded pay raise. The general increase in emoluments in 1960 was accompanied by a rise in the level of employment so that the total wage-bill went up from £G111.9 million in 1959 to £G136.4 million in 1960 or by about 22% [23]. The process of upward adjustment in wages and salaries continued during the first half of 1961 [24] when probably high-ranking government and private employees were the main beneficiaries. The wage-bill of the Government alone increased from £G17.6 million in 1960 to £G22.5 million in 1961 (appendix table XI). Although reliable estimates for the total wage-bill in 1961 are not available, there are indications that on the whole total gross earnings from employment increased at a slower rate than in the previous year. For example, average monthly money earnings per recorded employee (in all industries in the government and non-government sectors) rose by 4.3% between December 1960 and December 1961 as compared with 17.3% between December 1959 and December 1960 [25]. Contemporaneously with this

---

22 The minimum wage rate was raised to 6s. 6d. a day.

23 These figures exclude employees' earnings in private establishments employing less than 50 persons. Cf. *Economic Survey*, 1960, table 53, p. 59.

24 With the introduction of 1961/62 Budget in July 1961, the Government announced its "firm determination ... not to countenance any wage and salary increase". Cf. *Economic Survey*, 1961, p. 80. Following this announcement the Government and the Trades Union Congress reached a 'gentlemen's agreement' that there would be no wage increase during the course of the *Seven-Year Development Plan*. This agreement was adhered to up to the end of the period under review. It is also noteworthy that as a result of the initiative taken by the Congress, the workweek of civil servants and employees of statutory corporations was with effect from 1st April, 1962, increased from $39^{1}/_{2}$ to 42 hours, of which one hour could be taken off for shopping.

25 *Economic Survey*, 1962, table 75, p. 83. A closer look at the data on gross average earnings as published in the various issues of the *Economic Survey* raises serious doubts about their accuracy. It is for instance noteworthy that according to the *Economic Survey*, 1961 (table 68, p. 82), average earnings per

increase in wages and salaries, there was also an increase in the cocoa farmers' income. Due to favourable weather conditions, cocoa production during the 1960/61 season was about one-third higher than in 1959/60. Consequently, net income of the cocoa farmers went up from £G35.5 million in the 1959/60 crop season to £G48.3 million in the 1960/61 season (table 8). According to one reckoning, the total sum of money paid by the Cocoa Marketing Board to the cocoa farmers increased from £G37.9 million in 1959 to £G45.2 million in 1960 or by about 18%[26]. It is noteworthy that despite a sharp increase in money incomes the general price level (GNP deflator) in 1960 fell by 0.5% (appendix table III). The index of market prices for locally produced foodstuffs was on average two points lower in 1960 than in 1959[27]. In contrast, the average index of retail prices for Accra registered a modest increase of 0.8%[28]. Admittedly these indices are far from perfect[29]. Still, there can be little doubt about the broad conclusion that, the significant increase in money incomes notwithstanding, the prices on the whole showed a remarkable stability in 1960. Price stability during a period of rising money incomes may at first appear somewhat odd. But there is no real mystery here. The decline in the prices of locally produced foodstuffs — an important determinant of the general price level in a developing country like Ghana — was a direct result of an increase in the flow of these items (maize, yams, cassava, rice and millet) to the urban markets, partly because favourable weather conditions led to an increase in their production and, perhaps more importantly, due to the increased construction of feeder roads. Another factor in the relative stability of the general price level in 1960 was the virtual constancy of the import price index[30], on the one hand, and the increased availability of imported consumer goods, on the other[31]. But probably the most important reason why despite a significant increase in the

employee in 1961 were 12.8% higher than in 1960. In the *Economic Survey,* 1962, this figure was revised drastically to 4.3%. Similarly, whereas according to the *Economic Survey,* 1962 (table 75, p. 83), average earnings per employee rose by 4.6% between the end of 1961 and 1962, in the *Economic Survey,* 1963 (table 85, p. 119), the same figure was raised to 9.1%. Since the Central Bureau of Statistics never mentioned the reasons for these discrepancies, we have little choice but to consider the figure given in the later issue to be more authentic than the one published in the earlier issue.

26 *Bank of Ghana Report,* June 1961, p. 17.

27 *Economic Survey,* 1960, table 13, p. 25.

28 *Ibid.,* table 57, p. 62.

29 For instance, the retail price index for Accra was based on the 1954 consumption pattern of manual and related workers, i.e., workers earning up to £G180 per annum. It is highly unlikely that between 1954 and 1960 there was no change in the consumption habits of such workers.

30 The import price index rose by 0.4% between 1959 and 1960 (appendix table XIII).

31 The total volume of imports increased from £G126 million in 1959 to £148 million in 1960, i.e., by about 17% (appendix table I).

money incomes the prices remained stable in 1960 was that the increase in private consumption lagged behind the increase in money incomes. We have already noted the time-lag which exists between the cocoa farmers' receipts and expenditures. The phenomenon, however, appears to be of a general nature in the sense that there is usually a lag between the period over which income is received and the period over which it is spent[32]. That the additional purchasing power injected into the economy in 1960 did not lead to an equivalent increase in private consumption is evident from the fact that whereas during the year the total wage-bill and the cocoa farmers' net receipts increased respectively by £G24.5 million and £G7.3 million, private consumption expenditure went up by only £G22 million (appendix table I). This indicates that a not inconsiderable part of the additional money incomes in 1960 leaked out into idle cash balances implying an increase in the voluntary savings of the recipients. The foregoing analysis suggests that the increase in monetary ratio in 1960 in part reflected the building-up of additional idle cash balances in the wake of rising money incomes, on the one hand, and price stability, on the other.

The slightly more than 9% rise in the monetary ratio in 1961 — the highest rate of increase during the six-year period under review — occurred under entirely different circumstances. Although, as mentioned earlier, there was probably a further increase in money incomes especially during the first half of the year, it appears highly unlikely that postponement of consumption expenditure was the major factor in the increase in monetary ratio in 1961. In fact, private consumption expenditure rose significantly during the first half of the year when apparently there was a tendency to expand consumption at the cost of idle cash balances built up during the closing months of 1960. Another factor responsible for the significant increase in the internal demand in the first half of 1961 was the sharp rise in government expenditure to £G70 million as compared with £G47 million in the first half of 1960[33]. Meanwhile, largely due to adverse weather conditions, the production of local foodstuffs suffered a serious setback. Consequently, the increased internal demand in the first half of 1961 exerted a strong pressure on imports, which rose to £G75 million as compared with £G63 million in the corresponding period in 1960[34]. At the same time, a sharp fall in cocoa price in the world market reduced foreign exchange receipts from cocoa despite a significant increase in the volume exported. These developments led to a marked deterioration in the balance of payments position; between the end of

32 "It takes a certain time before production costs paid out as income are expended on consumption goods, and it may again take a certain time before these outlays become income again." Erik LUNDBERG: *Studies in the Theory of Economic Expansion,* Basil Blackwell, Oxford, 1955, p. 52.
33 *Economic Survey,* 1961, p. 22.
34 *Ibid.,* p. 116.

December 1960 and the end of June 1961 the country's external reserves fell sharply by nearly £G31 million to £G118.1 million[35].

To stem a further drain on the country's external reserves, in July 1961 the Government undertook a number of measures. Important among these were the introduction of an 'austerity' budget and a new exchange control law. The 1961/62 Budget had two main objectives: first, to raise additional revenue to meet proposed increase in government expenditure; and, second, to contain the private demand, especially for imported non-essential goods. To this end, the new budget, *inter alia*, (a) extended the coverage and increased the rates of import duties; (b) widened the personal income tax net, abolished the personal allowances, raised the tax rates and instituted the 'Pay As You Earn' system; (c) imposed a purchase tax on a number of consumer durables and luxury goods at rates ranging from 10 to 66.6%; and, (d) introduced a compulsory saving scheme requiring wage and salary earners, companies, and cocoa farmers to 'invest' a part of their incomes in the 4% National Development Bonds redeemable after 10 years[36].

Under the new exchange control regulations, which came into effect on 5th July, 1961, exchange control was extended to transactions with all countries including the sterling area[37], restrictions on invisibles and capital payments were in certain cases tightened and strict measures were introduced to check evasion. The Foreign Exchange Act, 1961, also stipulated that the commercial banks and insurance companies hold only limited balances abroad[38]. In addition, remittances of incomes by non-Ghanaians were restricted to 50% or £G2,500, whichever was less[39].

---

35 *Bank of Ghana Report,* June 1962, p. 17.
36 Under the scheme, which was introduced on Professor N. KALDOR's advice, the contributions were fixed at the following rate:
- wage and salary earners earning between £G108 and £G120 per annum = £G3;
- employees earning more than £G120 per annum = 5% of chargeable income;
- companies = 10% of chargeable income; and,
- cocoa farmers = 10% of price paid by the Cocoa Marketing Board.

The introduction of the scheme led to an 'unofficial' strike of railway and dock workers in the Sekondi-Takoradi area in September 1961. Although the scheme was abolished with effect from 1st November 1963, the cocoa farmers continued to pay the 10% levy as income tax.
37 Before 5th July, 1961, exchange control in Ghana was applied only to transactions with countries outside the sterling area.
38 Initially the commercial banks were required to hold not more than £G500,000 each in the form of external assets. At a later stage, the £G500,000 limit was abolished and the banks were required to hold the minimum necessary for their day-to-day transactions.
39 Previously the maximum amount an expatriate could transfer abroad was determined on an *ad hoc* basis and was in general much higher.

By and large, these measures failed to accomplish their purpose. The fiscal measures did not lead to any immediate reduction in the private demand. On the contrary, throughout the second half of the year the private demand, especially for imported consumer goods, continued to run at a high level. The pressure of demand in the economy was further intensified by an increase in government expenditure both on current and capital accounts. The sharp rise in aggregate demand was met by higher imports and reduction of stocks of consumer goods. Despite the higher import duties and purchase tax, there was an increase in the import of durable consumer goods such as radio sets, refrigerators, sewing machines, etc. Imports during the second half of 1961 amounted to £G67.6 million as compared with £G66.5 million in the corresponding period of 1960[40]. The increase of £G11 million in stocks in 1960 was rapidly used up and by the end of 1961 there was a further decline in stocks of £G10 million (appendix table I). On both these grounds, the rise in internal demand as such did not exert any significant and persistent pull on the general price level. Although during the year the average index of retail prices (for Accra only) increased by nearly 7% and the index of prices for locally produced foodstuffs went up by about 13%[41], much of the rise in the two indices could be attributed respectively to the increase in indirect taxation and the decline in production of local foodstuffs between March and August resulting from poor weather conditions. That despite the significant rise in internal demand and the sharp increase in indirect taxation the inflationary pressures did not gather any dangerous momentum is evident from the fact that during the year the general price index rose by only 3.3% over its level in 1960 (appendix table III).

The large imports and the significant decline in stocks of consumer goods were, however, not the only factors in stemming inflationary forces. Three further causes of the absence of strong and continuous pressure on prices in the second half of 1961 were: firstly, the tendency among the firms to sell existing stocks of durable consumer goods at the pre-budget prices[42], secondly, the introduction of price control to ensure stabilization of prices for essential commodities like flour, sugar, tea, common soap, tinned fish, kerosene, etc.[43], and, finally, the improvement in the overall food situation from September

---

40 *Economic Survey*, 1961, p. 116.
41 *Ibid.*, table 70, p. 84, and table 71, p. 86.
42 *Ibid.*, p. 23 .
43 Soon after the introduction of the 1961/62 Budget, the prices of these and certain other items of daily consumption went up significantly. The rise in the prices was in many cases out of proportion to the increase in import and excise duties imposed by the new budget. The Government therefore found it necessary to fix maximum prices for a number of essential commodities and made it obligatory on shopkeepers to display the full list of control prices prominently. *Ibid.*, p. 85.

onwards resulting from an increase in the supply of locally produced food-stuffs owing to improved weather conditions [44].

The sharp increase in imports in 1961, on the one hand, served to limit the inflationary pressures in the economy and, on the other, led to serious strains on the balance of payments. The current account deficit in the balance of payments increased from £G38.7 million in 1960 to £G52.7 million in 1961. At the same time, in part because of the new method of cocoa financing and in part due to government long term loans to Mali, Upper Volta and Guinea [45] as well as the purchase of certain foreign-owned gold mines, there was a net outflow of capital of about £G18 million (appendix table V). The combined effect of these developments was a sharp reduction in the country's foreign reserves by £G74.8 million to £G73.8 million — that is, to nearly half the level at the end of 1960 (appendix table IV).

It seems that the spectacular rise in the monetary ratio in 1961 was the result mainly of what may be termed as autonomous changes in the money national income and the money supply. During the year, while the rate of growth in current prices fell (from 7% in 1960) to 6.6%, the money supply rose by 16.3% over its level in the previous year. The slowdown in the pace of economic growth stemmed in part from a serious deterioration in the terms of trade owing to a sharp drop in the world cocoa price resulting in a decline in export proceeds from £G123 million in 1960 to £G122 million in 1961 (appendix table I). Another important factor in the decline of rate of growth of GNP was a slowdown of investment in manufacturing both in the public and private sectors. In the former sector this was a direct result of the suspension of the *Second Five-Year Plan* and the liquidation of the Industrial Development Corporation [46]. The slowdown in the private sector resulted from the uncertainties about the Government's attitude towards private enterprise created largely through the publication by the ruling political party, the CPP, of a policy document entitled "A Programme of Work and Happiness"

---

44 The index of market prices for locally produced foodstuffs (1954 = 100) fell from 148 in August to 135 in September and remained virtually stable in the last quarter of the year. *Ibid.*, table 71, p. 86.

45 It is noteworthy that in selling U.K. Government securities for the purpose of making these loans, Ghana obtained some £G2 million to £G3 million less than the nominal value of these securities.

46 The Industrial Development Corporation (I.D.C.) was established in 1947 to serve as an intermediary between the Central Government and the final project. By the end of June 1961, the Government had made about £G7 million available to the IDC in the form of *ad hoc* budgetary allocations. This sum was utilized by the IDC for investment in 31 industrial establishments of which 22 were fully owned by it. The liquidation of the IDC became necessary in view of mounting operational losses resulting from incompetent management. Following the disbandment of the IDC, in 1962 its assets and functions were transferred to a newly created Ministry of Industries. In mid-1964, the responsibility for these projects was transferred to a newly established State Enterprises Secretariat.

76

declaring socialism as the goal of the nation. Even though it was not until July 1962 that the Programme was formally adopted by the CPP, its very publication led to wild speculations and rumours about the Government's intention to block and confiscate all private savings and to nationalize foreign private enterprises. Although by and large these fears proved to be unfounded, they tended to discourage private investment with the result that the rate of increase of gross domestic capital formation fell sharply from nearly 26% in 1960 to less than 8% in 1961 (appendix table I).

The main factors generating the expansion of the money supply were the increase in bank credit to the Government and the non-government sector, in roughly equal amounts (table 3). The rise in the domestic credit operations of the banking system was attributable to a large number of unrelated developments. To begin with, as mentioned earlier, the year 1961 saw the introduction of a fiduciary issue. Secondly, the Bank of Ghana for the first time lent money to the Government in the form of Ways and Means Advances. These transactions of the central bank were reflected in a sharp rise in the currency in circulation. Thirdly, rising imports raised the demand for loans and advances in the wholesale and retail sectors. Finally, the imposition of exchange controls probably forced certain foreign firms to obtain credit locally rather than in countries of their origin. The expansionary effect of the exchange control regulations on the money supply was, however, by no means limited to the demand side. The stipulation that the commercial banks must maintain only minimum external balances led to the repatriation of large sums of money that were previously invested abroad. As a result, the commercial banks were induced to seek local avenues of investment for these funds.

The above factors help to explain a major part of the sudden marked increase in liquidity in the economy in 1961. Yet another explanation is probably to be found in the building-up of 'idle' demand deposits with the commercial banks in the wake of restrictions on remittances of incomes by non-Ghanaians. Though precise figures are not available, it seems likely that the stringent regulations and procedural delays tended to serve as important restraints on such transfers, forcing affected persons to hold more funds in the local currency than they actually required for their immediate commitments. And, to the extent that the rise in the demand deposits with the commercial banks was due to these restrictions, foreign exchange controls exercised a deflationary effect by increasing the liquidity in the economy.

The year 1962 opened with uncertainties surrounding the intentions of the Government concerning the development of the economy in general and the role of private enterprise in particular. On the one hand, the budgetary and exchange control measures of the preceding year began to make their full impact on the economy. On the other hand, the incessant use of fancy slogans about socialism by high-ranking party and government officials weakened the confidence of the private business community in the future of the Ghanaian economy. In the first half of the year there was a further slow-down of economic activity as a result of a decrease in private and government expenditures both on consumption and fixed investment. One strategic factor in the decline in aggregate demand was the introduction of specific licensing system on 1st December, 1961. Resort to licensing mechanism was found necessary because past experience had shown that due to the high marginal propensity to import customs duties were not sufficiently effective in curtailing the volume of imports and hence in arresting a continuous diminution in the country's foreign reserves. The new import policy aided by the stringent exchange controls and increase in taxes led to some gratifying results. In 1962, the current account deficit in the balance of payments fell sharply to £G28.2 million, i.e., to almost half the size of the preceding year. This spectacular decline in the level of external deficit coupled with the inflow of official and private capital and a drawing of £G5 million from the I.M.F. (in August) prevented a further drain on the external reserves, which at the end of 1962 remained almost at the same level as at the end of 1961 (appendix tables IV and V).

Another explanation for the considerably low level of investment in 1962 is to be found in the new official policy towards industry announced by the President on 24th March, 1962. Under the new scheme, the economy was to be divided into the following five sectors, all operating side by side: (a) the state sector; (b) the foreign private sector; (c) the joint state-foreign private sector; (d) the cooperative sector; and (e) the small-scale private sector. The last two sectors were in principle reserved for Ghanaians but foreign firms already established in the fifth sector were to continue operation provided they did not expand their existing scale of operation. What, however, made the new policy really suspect in the eyes of foreign private enterprises were the two stipulations attached to their continued existence. The first was that in case of sale of all or part of their equity capital the foreign private enterprises were to give the Government of Ghana the first option to buy these shares. The second stipulation was that all foreign private enterprises (as well as all those jointly owned by the state and foreign private interests) must reinvest 60% of their net profits (i.e., after the payment of income and withholding taxes[47]) in Ghana[48]. While the 'first option' condition aroused fear of nationalization, the stringent restrictions on transfer of profits discouraged new foreign investors. Although, as subsequently became apparent, the new policy was not designed to hinder the operation and growth of the private sector, it raised serious doubts about the ambit for operation and the security of foreign private enterprise in Ghana. To allay

47 At the rate of 40% and 2.5% respectively.
48 Previously the entire amount of net profits could be transferred.

78

these apprehensions, in June 1962 the Government gave a categorical assurance that its policy on transfer of profits was not a rigid one and that it would be willing to make special arrangements with firms operating in fields which in its view were productive. It was also clarified that: (a) the 60% reinvestment requirement was inclusive of the 10% contribution towards the Compulsory Savings Scheme; (b) the Government would not in any way hinder foreign firms from remitting 40% of their net profits abroad; and, (c) in the event of more than 60% of net profit being reinvested in any one year, appropriate allowances would be made in the next year. Parallel with these assurances and clarifications an attempt was made to streamline some of the fiscal measures introduced in July 1961. In particular, with the introduction of 1962/63 Budget in October 1962, the Purchase Tax Act, 1961, was greatly amended with a view to remove certain anomalies[49]. In addition, purchase tax rates on commercial vehicles and certain imported durable consumer goods such as refrigerators, cookers, washing machines, radios, were considerably reduced.

In view of these assurances and concessions, there was during the second half of 1962 some revival of private investment. Yet, on the whole, private business community continued to display, what the *Economic Survey*, 1962, called, an attitude of "caution" and "wait-and-see" (p. 21). And, as mentioned earlier, the overall investment during the year remained considerably below the level attained in the years 1960 and 1961.

The main stimulus to economic activity in 1962 was government consumption expenditure which rose by as much as 11%. Private consumption expenditure on the other hand showed only a modest increase of 3.2%. However, allowing for the price increases, private consumption in real terms dropped by about 6% between 1961 and 1962, as against a rise of 9.6% in the real consumption in the government sector (appendix table I). In per capita terms, the decline in real consumption in the private sector was even larger because of the increase in population of nearly 3%. This means that while fiscal measures and accompanying import restrictions and exchange controls put a serious brake on private consumption, the Government preferred to increase its own consumption expenditure. It is noteworthy that even though due to a vigorous tax effort tax receipts showed considerable improvements over the level in 1961, the rise in government expenditure, notably on consumption, outstripped the increase in current revenue (appendix table XIV). The Government's financial intemperance in 1962 is evident from the fact that of the total budget deficit of about £G46 million nearly one-third was financed by borrowing from the banking system.

---

49 For example, to rectify the anomaly by which purchase tax on expensive cars with efficient smaller engine was lower than on inexpensive cars with bigger engine, it was decided to shift the basis of the tax from cubic capacity of engine to landed cost.

It may seem surprising that even though deficit financing by the Government increased from £G8.5 million in 1961 to £G13.9 million in 1962, money supply in the latter year was only £G4.8 million higher than in the former year. The explanation for the slowdown in the rate of increase in money supply in 1962 (7.8% as against 12.8% in 1961) is to be found largely in the fact that during the year, owing to a sharp curtailment in private investment activity and significant restraint in private consumption, gross bank credit to the non-government sector remained virtually at the same level as in 1961 (appendix table IX). In fact, as can be seen from table 3, 1962 was the only year in which the non-government sector exercised a net contractionary effect on the money supply.

The restraint in private demand also prevented any excessive pressure being exerted on the price level. The general price level rose by 2.1% between 1961 and 1962 but this increase was more is the nature of an adjustment to the past inflationary pressures than due to new expansionary impulses. For instance, much of the nearly 9% increase in the average index of retail prices for Accra could be traced to the fact that with the depletion of the pre-budget (1961/62) stocks, the retail prices of durable consumer goods rose by the full amount of import duty and purchase tax. Similarly, the approximately 8% rise in the index of market prices for locally produced foodstuffs was largely attributable to adverse weather conditions, which disrupted the supplies to the consuming centre, and to the increase in freight rates resulting from higher taxes on vehicles and spares[50].

In 1963, the falling trend in private consumption was reversed; but more significant was the rise in gross domestic fixed capital formation, which went up by 18.4% over the level in 1962. This marked increase in investment partly reflected the rise in government development expenditure, especially on the Volta River Project, for which the financial arrangements were completed in 1962. In part, the rise in capital formation was also due to the increased investment activity in the private sector. Private investment in 1963 increased both because of the further liberalization in the Government policy towards private enterprise and because of the relaxation of import controls on machinery and equipment.

Although in general the official economic policy continued to have socialistic overtones, with the completion of the draft of the *Seven-Year Development Plan* in early 1963, the Government shifted to a more positive attitude towards private enterprise. This change of mood was reflected both in the enactment of the Capital Investments Act in April, and the establishment of the National Investment Bank in June. Under the Capital Investments Act both foreign and domestic private investors were offered generous fiscal concessions, a number of other inducements and benefits and, above all,

---

50 *Economic Survey*, 1962, pp. 83–87.

statutory protection against nationalization without adequate compensation[51]. The National Investment Bank, on the other hand, was charged with the promotion of productive enterprises in the private sector by providing medium and long term loans together with managerial and technical assistance and advice. In brief, the main functions of the Bank were: (a) to assist in the establishment, improvement, expansion and modernization of enterprises; (b) to counsel and encourage small Ghanaian business concerns; (c) to encourage and facilitate the participation of internal and external capital in such enterprises; and, (d) to bring together investment opportunities, internal and external capital, and experienced management.

These gestures of goodwill and accommodation were followed by further fiscal concessions granted in October 1963. The 1963/64 Budget not only abolished the Compulsory Savings Scheme[52], but, more significantly, it also repealed the 60% reinvestment rule for foreign enterprises. And, even though at the same time the rates of company income tax and withholding tax were raised to 45% and 20% respectively, on the whole from the point of view of foreign investors the new arrangements were admittedly a significant improvement over the previous situation.

As already mentioned, another factor in the recovery of investment activity in the private sector was the Government's decision to place greater emphasis on the import of producers' equipment and raw materials. Consequently, in 1963 imports of capital equipment and raw and semifinished materials amounted to £G71.7 million, a rise of 32% from the level in 1962[53]. In the face of this marked increase in the import of investment goods and a further decline in export earnings the imbalance in the country's external trade and payments position deteriorated. In 1963, the current account deficit rose to

---

51 To administer these provisions, a Capital Investments Board was set up. Investment projects approved by the Board could be given all or some of the following concessions: a) an income tax holiday for a period up to ten years from the date of production; b) special capital allowance for a period up to five years; c) exemption from all indirect taxation including custom duties, excise duties, purchase tax, etc.; d) exemption from property tax and similar taxes; e) exemption from restrictions on transfer abroad of principal, interest or profits on foreign investment; f) facilities to expatriate staff for remittances abroad in respect of the maintenance of their families and contractual obligations such as contributions to provident and pension funds, insurance premiums, etc.; and, g) guarantee of compensation in case of nationalization and provision for international arbitration in cases of disagreement between the Government and private investors.

52 In case of companies and self-employed persons the abolition was with retroactive effect from the first of July, 1963. The contributions already made for the period from July to October were to be set off against income tax payments.

53 Imports of consumer goods, on the other hand, fell from £G55.9 million in 1962 to £G51.4 million in 1963. *Cf. Economic Survey*, 1964, table 13, p. 39, and *Economic Survey*, 1966, table 13, p. 31.

£G45.7 million and there was a further drain on the external reserves to the tune of £G29.1 million (appendix table V).

Even though the fall in foreign exchange assets was a contractionary factor, the rate of monetary expansion picked up again. The rise in money supply in 1963 amounted to £G8.4 million as compared with the rise of £G4.8 million in the preceding year (appendix table II). Unlike 1962 when the government sector was primarily responsible for the increase in money supply, the expansionary influence in 1963 came partly from the non-government sector (table 3). A higher level of private investment, increased quantum of imports, and the introduction of a new method of financing the cocoa crop (i.e., internally) necessitated a significant stepping up in bank lending to the non-government sector. Partly to the same factors must be traced the rise in the monetary ratio in 1963.

Under the impact both of an increase in the budgetary gap and a rise in private expenditure on consumption and investment, a substantial rise occurred in the total effective demand. On the other hand, despite a significant increase in domestic manufacturing production (table 9), there was a decline in goods availabilities, in part due to the restricted imports of consumer goods and in part owing to a shortfall in the supply of local foodstuffs. The shortages of local foodstuffs emerged mainly due to the bottlenecks in distribution system, created by heavy rains and floods. Consequently, in 1963 the price situation came under heavy pressure, and between March and December the national price index and the index of market prices of local foodstuffs (for urban areas) on average went up by 8.6% and 5.9% respectively[54], reflecting in a rise of 6.9% in the general price index (appendix table III).

The year 1964 marked yet another turning point in the Government's import policy. Alarmed by the critically low level to which the foreign reserves had by then fallen, the Government entered upon a policy of tighter import control in 1964. Early in the year all valid specific import licences were abruptly withdrawn, and in the subsequent exercise of re-issue an attempt was made to curtail the volume of import of consumer goods, especially non-essential items. Though in the final analysis the total merchandise import bill was in 1964 only £G5 million lower than in 1963 (appendix table V), the critical point was that the import of consumer goods was severely curtailed. That the onus of new import restrictions fell almost exclusively on non-durable and durable consumer goods can be seen from the fact that their imports fell

---

54 *Economic Survey*, 1963, tables XXVI and XXVII, pp. 152–153. On the basis of the information obtained from a national household budget survey (covering households with an income of £G600 or less per annum) conducted in 1961, the Central Bureau of Statistics compiled the new all-Ghana indices for consumer prices as well as for prices of locally produced foodstuffs with March 1963 as base.

from some £G51 million in 1963 to about £G41 million in 1964, i.e., by 20%[55].

There was during the year probably some increase in the production of local foodstuffs. However, owing to the lack of vehicles and spare parts, whose imports fell by 50% between 1963 and 1964[56], the road transport system developed serious bottlenecks and the supplies to the urban markets were substantially reduced. Domestic manufacturing production rose significantly over its level in the previous year (table 9) but could not compensate for the loss of imports apparently because its poor quality limited the possibilities of substitution between home and foreign goods.

Another factor in the growing shortages of consumer goods, especially of foreign origin, was the hoarding of goods by the wholesale dealers and retailers. The hoarding activities in 1964 can be attributed to two factors. First, embarrassed by the growing complaints about the rapid upward march of prices and rampant black marketing, the Government extended the controlled price list, strengthened the price inspection system and announced severe penalties for black marketing. The evidence is, however, strong that these measures did not prove effective. Paradoxically, they tended to aggravate the shortages and raise the prices, for the fear of prosecution probably encouraged the sellers to withhold the supplies and to devise more subtle methods of black marketing. Secondly, there were growing apprehensions that the next budget — which was originally to be announced in October but eventually postponed by 3 months by changing the fiscal year to coincide with the calendar year — would bring about even tighter import restrictions and higher import duties. Such speculations raised the tempo of hoarding activity with the result that in the last quarter of 1964 some essential consumer goods virtually disappeared from the open market.

The mounting shortages of consumer goods apparently served as a restraint on private consumption expenditure in 1964. Unable to find sufficient goods in the open market at 'reasonable' prices, the consumers were forced to postpone consumption and accumulate idle cash balances. Thus, during the year, whereas private consumption in real terms fell to £G358.5 million from £G372 million in 1963, i.e., by 3.6% (appendix table I), less-liquid desposits of the 'public' with the commercial banks rose by £G7.7 million (appendix table IX).

In this connection mention must also be made of the fact that in 1964 the Central Bureau of Statistics found it difficult to obtain information on the 'true' price situation. As a result, the price indices compiled by the Bureau

55 *Economic Survey,* 1964, table IX, p. 125.
56 *Ibid.*

were largely based on the controlled, i.e., minimum, prices[57]. To the extent that these price indices were used for estimating private consumption expenditure, the figure of the GNP in current prices for 1964 issued by the Bureau and used in this study is lower than the one which would have been obtained by using the 'actual' prices. Hence, the increase in money-income ratio, given the money supply, appears to be greater than it actually was. It is therefore likely that the increase in prices in 1964 actually absorbed a somewhat greater proportion of the total credit monetization than is suggested by the figure given in table 5 and appendix table VI. Insofar as this is true, a part of the increase in the monetary liquidity in 1964 is merely a statistical illusion. This qualification, though necessary and relevant, does not impair the above conclusion that forced savings was an important element in the expansion of monetary ratio in 1964.

In part, the significant expansion in the monetary liquidity in 1964 must also be traced to the exceptionally large cocoa crop during the 1964/65 season (table 8) and the withdrawal of Ghana, together with the other members of the Cocoa Producers' Alliance, from the world market in October[58]. On both these grounds, there was in the last quarter of the year a significant increase in bank credit for cocoa financing. The hold-up of sales led to an accumulation of cocoa stocks which needed additional funds to hold[59].

The building-up of idle balances and the forced postponement of consumption implied by it, however, proved short-lived. By the beginning of 1965 consumers had become increasingly conscious of the inflationary pressures and fearful of further rises in prices. That these fears were not idle became apparent in February 1965, when the new budget was announced. By far the most important feature of the 1965 Budget was the introduction of a single-stage sales tax of 11.5% on practically all imported and locally manufactured goods and a large variety of services[60]. Since the economy was already running on a tight-rope, the tax had an immediate impact on the price level; the national consumer price index (March 1963 = 100) rose from 128

---

57 "... because of the fear of prosecutions under the price control laws, retailers... attempt to quote the control prices to price collectors of the Bureau unless they feel that they are not dealing with price inspectors." *Economic Survey*, 1965, p. 101.

58 *See*, chapter I, footnote 33.

59 Almost all the £G7 million increase in stocks (in current prices) in 1964 was due to the building up of cocoa stocks. *See*, appendix table I.

60 The sales tax was originally intended as a 10% tax on articles exchanged between a wholesale dealer and a retail trader or between two wholesale dealers. *Cf. Sales Tax Act*, 1965 (Act 257). It was, however, soon realized that because most retail traders in Ghana keep no records, it would be difficult to administer a multiple-stage sales tax. Consequently, in less than a fortnight the Bill was amended to exempt retail sales from the tax. At the same time, in order to make up the loss of revenue involved in this amendment, the rate of the tax was increased to 11.5%.

in January to 163 in July — an increase of roughly 27⁰/₀ over a period of six months[61].

It appears that with the intensification of inflationary pressures the tendency towards exchanging idle cash balances for goods became widespread — a move which in turn might have accelerated the inflationary process. The decision to run down idle balances was probably also influenced by the widespread rumours that the Government might combine the introduction of decimal currency in July with a devaluation of the currency. The process of transforming money holdings into goods accentuated in the second half of the year when "to please those attending the O.A.U. meeting" the shops were filled with imported consumer goods. It is noteworthy that despite the severe shortage of foreign exchange then facing the country there was a substantial increase in the issue of import licences culminating in an all time record current account deficit of £G81.5 million (appendix table V). The import of consumer goods alone went up by £G14 million over its level in the previous year to £G55 million[62], and it is reasonable to assume that the consumers seized this opportunity to get rid of at least a part of their unwanted money balances[63].

The above factors help to explain why despite a much higher increase in the money supply, on the one hand, and virtually no increase in the real GNP, on the other, the net expansion in the monetary liquidity in 1965 was substantially less than in 1964.

8. Domestic Production Growth

As we noted earlier, increase in domestic production on the whole absorbed a relatively small portion of the total monetary expansion. The gross national product at constant prices (1960 = 100) increased from £G439.5 million in 1959 to £G546.5 million in 1965. The increase in real gross national product during the six-year period 1960—65 was 24.3⁰/₀ as against an estimated population increase of 19⁰/₀[64].

---

61 *Economic Survey*, 1965, table XXXVI, p. 148–149.
62 *Economic Survey*, 1966, table 13, p. 31.
63 Note, however, that from individual's point of view the running down of money balances was in the short run not necessarily an act of dissaving. It is probably more appropriate to look at this exercise as an attempt to switch over from one form of hoarding to another.
64 According to the census conducted in 1960 Ghana in that year had a population of 6.7 million. Since then the population is estimated to have increased at an annual rate of 2.7–3.0⁰/₀. The data on per capita income published in the *Economic Survey*, 1966, reveal that by the end of 1965 Ghana's population had increased to 7.7 million. *See*, appendix table I.

Table 8. Cocoa Production, Export, Export Receipts and Cocoa Farmers' Income, 1960—65

	1960	1961	1962	1963	1964	1965
1. Cocoa Crop [a] (thousand long tons)	317	432	410	422	421	572
2. Cocoa Export (thousand long tons)	297	405	421	405	382	494
3. Export Receipts (£G million)	65.4	69.3	67.0	68.1	68.1	68.2
4. Average Price Per Long Ton (£G) (line 3 / line 2)	220	171	159	168	178	138
5. Index of Average Price (1960 = 100)	100	78	72	76	81	63
6. Relative Share of Cocoa Receipts in Total Exports Earnings (%)	55.0	61.1	60.0	63.3	60.7	61.1
7. Gross Producer Price Per Long Ton [a] (£G)	134.4	134.4	134.4	134.4	112.0	112.0
8. Net Producer Price Per Long Ton [a] (£G)	112.0	100.8	100.8	100.8	100.8	100.8
9. Net Income of Cocoa Farmers [a] (£G million)	35.5	48.25	41.25	42.55	42.45	57.65

[a] These figures are for the cocoa crop years. Thus, for example, the figure shown under 1960 relates to the period from October 1959 to September 1960. The net producer price represents the amount paid per long ton by the Cocoa Marketing Board net of voluntary contributions (introduced in May 1959 a £G22/8/– per ton and in effect abolished in September 1963 when the gross producers' price was reduced by an equal amount), and compulsory savings (introduced in July 1961 a £G 11/4/– per long ton; after 1962/63 compulsory savings were designated 'cocoa farmers' 'income tax').

Sources: Economic Survey, 1962, table 11, p. 33.
 Economic Survey, 1964, tables 15 and 16, pp. 43 and 45.
 Economic Survey, 1966, tables 15, 16 and 20, pp. 33, 34 and 46.

The ostensibly modest increase in the real national income, however, hides the significant fact that the six-year period under review was characterized by a marked expansion in cocoa production as well as in the output of large-scale manufacturing. As can be seen from table 8, cocoa production increased from 317,000 long tons in 1959/60 to 572,000 long tons in 1964/65, i.e., by 80%. Note that in 1964/65 cocoa production went up by 36% over its level in 1963/64. The phenomenal increase in cocoa production in 1964/65 can be attributed to a variety of factors. Important among these were: first, the exceptionally favourable weather conditions, and second, the coming into bearing of high-yield cocoa trees planted in the '50s when the world price of cocoa was high.

The growth of large-scale manufacturing since 1962 is indicated by the following table[65]:

Table 9. Gross Manufacturing Production[a], 1962—65

(In 1962 Fixed Prices)

Year	Value of Gross Output (£G million)	Index
1962	35.7	100.0
1963	43.9	123.0
1964	47.4	132.7
1965	47.7	133.6

[a] Large-scale manufacturing establishments engaging 30 or more persons.
Source: Economic Survey, 1966, table 33, p. 61.

As can be seen from table 9, the rate of growth of manufacturing output slowed down from 23% in 1963 to 8% in 1964 and dropped to 0.6% in 1965. The main cause for the slow expansion in 1964 and the virtual stagnation in 1965 was the growing shortage of raw materials and spare parts occasioned by the bottlenecks in import licensing system. The manufacturing industries most severely hit by these shortages were leather, non-metallic mineral products, transport equipment, and furniture and fixtures. Food, beverages, tobacco, textile and chemicals manufacturing industries, on the other hand, showed considerable increases in their outputs throughout the period 1962–65[66]. On the whole, the share of large-scale manufacturing in

---

65 Data on manufacturing production before 1962 are not available. Statistics on industrial production were for the first time collected in 1962 when a full-scale industrial census covering practically the whole country was conducted by the Central Bureau of Statistics.
66 For further details, see, Economic Survey, 1966, table 42, p. 68.

gross national product (in current prices) is estimated to have increased from 4.4⁰/₀ in 1960 to close to 8⁰/₀ in 1965 [67].

In contrast to the spectacular expansion in cocoa production and the growth of the manufacturing sector, production of local foodstuffs during the period under review appears to have lagged far behind the demands of the growing population [68]. The deficiency in food production was occasionally accentuated by the failure of crops due to adverse weather conditions. Adverse weather conditions, however, do not seem to have been the major factor in the relative stagnation of domestic food supply. Nor can the unsatisfactory trend in local food production be exclusively attributed to the lack of price incentives. Indeed, except for 1960 when, as we have seen, there was a significant decline in the prices of locally produced foodstuffs, the period under review was on the whole characterized by an upward trend in the wholesale and retail prices of local foodstuffs. For example, the wholesale price index of local foodstuffs (1961 = 100) moved up to 120.2 in December 1964 and by the end of 1965 rose to 163.8 [69].

The disappointing trend in the domestic food production can be partly explained by the indifferent attitude of the Government towards small-scale private farming and partly by the extremely slow increase in the agricultural labour force [70]. Due to its obsession with the large-scale mechanized state farming, the Government not only withdrew its support from peasant farmers but it also tended to starve them of even the most primitive tools and implements such as hoes, cutlasses, axes, etc. While huge sums were spent by the Government on land-clearing and import of tractors, the small-scale farmers found it increasingly difficult to buy seeds, fertilizers and insecticides at reasonable prices. At the same time, the introduction of compulsory free primary education in mid-1961 deprived the traditional agricultural sector of child labour. The loss of man-power was accentuated by the growing tendency

---

67 The Central Bureau of Statistics does not publish data on gross national product by sources of origin. The figures on the share of large-scale manufacturing in GNP are rough estimates and should be so treated.

68 Reliable data on food production in Ghana are not available. An agricultural census carried out by the Ministry of Agriculture in 1963 (first phase) and 1965 (second phase), however, revealed that during 1960–65 there was probably no increase in per capita output in the agricultural sector. On this assumption, STOCES has shown that food production in the period 1960–65 increased by only 1.4⁰/₀. However, by using the domestic food consumption expenditure approach, the same author arrived at a figure of 8.3⁰/₀. Accordingly, he concludes that the annual rate of increase in food production between 1960–65 ranged between 0.3 and 1.6⁰/₀. *See*, F. STOCES: "Agricultural Production in Ghana, 1955–65", *The Economic Bulletin of Ghana*, Vol. X (1966), No. 3.

69 *Economic Survey*, 1964, table 77, p. 110, and *Economic Survey*, 1965, table 76, p. 103.

70 F. STOCES, for instance, has estimated that during 1960–65 the agricultural labour force in Ghana increased by about 1.4⁰/₀. *op. cit.*, p. 9.

Table 10. **Food Imports, 1960—65**

Year	Food Imports (£G million)	Food Imports as % of Total Imports
1960	21.0	16.2
1961	26.3	18.3
1962	22.3	19.1
1963	18.5	14.2
1964	20.0	16.4
1965	17.6	11.0

Sources: *Economic Survey*, 1960, table 78, p. 84.
Economic Survey, 1964, table 12, p. 38.
Economic Survey, 1966, table 12, p. 30.

among the semi-educated teenagers to bid farewell to farming and to seek employment in the urban centres.

The failure of domestic food production to increase as fast as the population resulted in the emergence of food deficits. As can be seen from table 10, Ghana had to incur each year substantial foreign exchange expenditure on food imports. These large food imports bills were an important element in the persistent balance of payments disequilibrium.

9. Balance of Payments Developments

The six-year period under review was marked by persistent deficits on the current account of the balance of payments and a sharp decline in the foreign reserves. During 1960–65 the cumulative current account deficits amounted to £G280 million. The net foreign reserves which at the end of 1959 stood at £G166.7 million were during the next six years completely depleted. Meanwhile, net capital inflows rose and external debt increased from £G6 million at the end of 1959 to an estimated £G220 million at the end of 1965 (appendix table XVI).

The two main causes of this deterioration in the external balance were: (a) increase in imports, and, (b) persistent deterioration in the terms of trade. The upward pressures on imports were exerted, on the one hand, by the growing consumer demand and the large development expenditures by the Government and, on the other, by the disappointingly slow increase in domestic production. Imports increased rapidly in 1960 and again in 1961 when the duties were low and over 90% of the country's imports were under Open General Licence. With the imposition of heavy import duties and the virtual abolition of Open General Licence in December 1961, the level of imports came down significantly in 1962 relieving the pressure on the balance of payments. This relaxation, however, proved to be a temporary phenomenon. In the following year, imports surged up again turning the trade balance from a surplus of £G3.4 million in 1962 to a deficit of £G10.7 million in 1963. In 1964, by raising the level of import duties and imposing tighter import controls the Government managed to hold down the merchandise imports at a level exactly equal to that of exports. In 1965, however, owing to a dramatic increase in government current and capital expenditures imports rose to the highest ever recorded level of £G156 million intensifying the pressure on the balance of payments.

Table 11. **Balance of Payments Summary, 1960—65**
(£G million)

	1960	1961	1962	1963	1964	1965
1. Imports (f.o.b.)	124.3	137.4	110.8	120.3	114.9	156.2
2. Exports (f.o.b.)	119.2	118.8	114.2	109.6	114.8	114.7
3. Trade deficit (− = surplus)	5.1	18.6	−3.4	10.7	0.1	41.5
4. Services and transfer payments (net)	33.6	34.1	31.6	35.0	34.6	40.0
5. Deficit on current account	38.7	52.7	28.2	45.7	34.7	81.5
Financed by:						
6. Decrease in foreign reserves	18.1	74.8	1.4	29.1	12.4	33.0
7. Capital inflow (net)	29.0	−18.1	20.9	24.4	27.7	58.7
8. IMF Position (net)	–	–	5.1	–	–	−3.8
9. Errors and Omissions	−8.4	−4.0	0.8	−7.8	−5.4	−6.4

Source: Derived from appendix table V.

While imports were increasing, export receipts remained virtually stagnant. Ghana derives close to two-thirds of her foreign exchange earnings from export of cocoa. Although export of cocoa increased from 297,000 long tons in 1960 to 494,000 long tons in 1965, owing to a decline in the world price there was hardly any increase in the receipts. As can be seen from table 8, the index of average export price of cocoa (1960 = 100) fell by 37⁰/o over the six-year period 1960–65. As a result, the over-all index of exports prices declined from 100 in 1960 to 75 in 1965 (appendix table XIII). The losses from the decline in export prices were augmented in the last two years of the period under review when the import price index resumed its upward march[71]. Altogether, as a result of the deterioration in the terms of trade, between 1960–65 the country suffered a loss of real income of an estimated

---

71 It seems that the sharp upward trend in the import price index in 1964 and 1965 was to some extent caused by the false invoicing of imports as a means of circumventing the exchange control regulations.

£G150 million, of which about one-third occurred in 1965 alone (appendix table XIII).

Another implication of the decline in the world price of cocoa is worth noting. Because the Cocoa Marketing Board — the sole buying and selling agency — continued to pay a fixed price to the cocoa farmers, their money incomes did not fall *pari passu* with the downward trend in the world price[72]. That the producer price paid by the Board was heavily subsidised is evident from the fact that during the six-year period under review it incurred heavy trading losses and except for the fiscal years 1960/61 and 1963/64 failed to pay to the Government the voluntary contributions it collected from cocoa farmers. In fact, with a substantial part of its dwindling reserves locked up in loans to the Government, the Board had to borrow from the banking system to finance the purchases of cocoa from farmers. Thus, in the period in which the terms of trade were deteriorating, the price stabilization policy of the Board contributed to the high level of money incomes and, given the high marginal propensity to consume and the relative inelasticity of substitution between home and foreign goods, tended to intensify the pressures on balance of payments.

Table 12. **Composition of Imports by End-Use, 1959—65**
(Percentages)

	1959	1960	1961	1962	1963	1964	1965
1. Consumer goods (Non-durable and durable)	50.3	50.0	49.4	47.9	39.4	33.6	34.2
2. Raw and Semi-finished materials	26.0	23.9	27.7	28.3	30.4	34.0	31.5
3. Capital equipment[a]	18.8	21.6	18.7	18.2	24.7	26.7	30.2
4. Fuel and lubricants	4.9	4.5	4.2	5.6	5.5	5.7	4.0
Total Imports	100.0	100.0	100.0	100.0	100.0	100.0	100.0

[a] Including spare parts, but excluding ships, fishing trawlers and aircrafts (except one VC-10 aircraft imported in 1965).

Sources: Economic Survey, 1960, table 79, p. 86.
Economic Survey, 1963, table 13, p. 43.
Economic Survey, 1964, table 13, p. 39.
Economic Survey, 1966, table 13, p. 31.

Mention must also be made of the significant changes in the composition of imports during the period under review. As can be seen from table 12, in the period from 1960 to 1965 the share of consumer goods went down persistently from one-half to one-third, while that of capital equipment rose

72 In September, 1965, the gross producer price was reduced to £G74.65 per long ton.

from less than one-fifth to almost one-third. At the same time, the relative importance of raw and semi-finished materials increased continually; this group accounted for 31.5% of the total imports in 1965 as compared to 23.9% in 1960.

The significant increase in the shares of capital equipment and raw and semi-finished materials in the total imports reflects the Government's efforts to allocate an increasing share of the available foreign exchange resources to investment and thereby to increase the tempo of industrialization. That industrialization led to a rapid increase in the demand for imported raw materials is explained by the fact that most of the manufacturing enterprises completed during the period continued to depend on foreign supplies, partly because some of them were so conceived and partly because no serious efforts were made to initiate or expand the production of local substitutes.

One of the most striking features of the increase in the relative share of capital equipment in the total imports has been the increasing resort to suppliers' credits to finance such imports. This is evident from the fact that of the total imports of capital equipment during the six-year period 1960–65 (£G190 million), capital goods delivered under suppliers' credits accounted for no less than 43%[73]. Since the majority of these credits, especially from Western countries, were of medium term, the debt service charges (including amortization) increased rapidly and by the end of 1965 amounted to £G22.4 million, accounting for 19.5% of the total export receipts in that year (appendix table XVI).

---

73 Note that this figure relates to the recorded deliveries of capital goods under suppliers' credits as shown in the official balance of payments statement. *See,* appendix table V, and Ch. III, footnotes 10 and 11.

CHAPTER III

CAPITAL FORMATION AND ECONOMIC GROWTH IN GHANA

This chapter aims at examining the impact of deficit financing in the government sector on the level of real capital formation and the rate of growth of the economy. The saving and investment flows in Ghana during the period 1958–65 will be assessed, the overall investment level in real terms will be calculated, and the trends in real capital formation in the government and non-government sectors will be analyzed. It will be assumed that the ultimate aim of money creation by the Government was to divert real resources from consumption to investment and thereby to step up the rate of growth of the economy. The success of deficit financing as a policy instrument will therefore be judged in terms of trends in real consumption, investment and rate of economic growth. Finally, the causes of a falling rate of growth of the economy despite a rising rate of investment will be investigated, especially with reference to the nature and composition of government investment outlays.

1. Saving and Investment Flows in Ghana, 1958–65

We shall begin this section with a brief description of concepts, sources of data and methods of computation. As can be seen from appendix table I, the national accounts in Ghana are based on estimates of aggregate expenditure on goods and services compiled by the Central Bureau of Statistics[1]. It would be tedious to explain in detail the methods of imputation used by the Bureau to estimate the various components of the expenditure on the Gross Domestic Product and to discuss the accuracy of the data[2]. Suffice it

---

1 Although in recent years some attempts have been made to compute the GDP from production figures of certain sectors of the economy as well as on the basis of available income data, the national accounts in Ghana continue to be based essentially on estimates of aggregate expenditure on goods and services, classified by their final uses.

2 For a detailed discussion of the methods of computation and limitations, *see,* BIRMINGHAM, NEUSTADT, OMABOE (eds.), *op. cit.,* ch. 2.

to say that, despite some improvements in recent years [3], first, the coverage in some respects remains incomplete and, second, the methods of estimation continue to suffer from certain inherent flaws. It should be added, however, that in spite of a number of gaps and imperfections the data on the Gross Domestic Product compiled and published by the Bureau provide a fairly consistent record of the growth of the economy in the sense that both the extent of omission and the margin of error in calculations seem to have remained reasonably constant throughout the period.

For the purpose of the present analysis we have found it necessary to derive the key magnitudes of the saving and investment flows directly from the published data on the Gross Domestic Product. This, as we shall soon see, is a fairly simple task. What is, however, not easy is the presentation of these flows on a sectoral (government and non-government) basis. There are a number of conceptual problems and practical difficulties resulting partly from the lack of precise and uniform concepts of the government and non-government sectors and partly from the fact that the Central Bureau of Statistics publishes only overall figures of gross domestic capital formation. These problems and the various methods we have used to overcome them will become evident as we go along.

The method of computation of saving and investment flows which we are using here consists of two stages. The first stage is to derive the figures of total gross domestic savings and investment from the published data on expenditure on the Gross Domestic Product in current prices. The second stage is to divide total gross domestic savings and investment between the government and non-government sectors.

Table 13 shows the sources and uses of investment funds in current prices for the period 1958–65. On the uses side, the figures for gross domestic fixed investment (item III) and increase in stocks (item IV) are taken directly from the published data on expenditure on the Gross Domestic Product in current prices (i.e., from appendix table I). On the sources side, the figures for excess of imports of goods and non-factor services over exports of goods and non-factor services (item II) are also taken from the published data on the GDP in current prices [4]. Gross domestic savings (item I) are calculated by sub-

---

3 For instance, on the basis of data collected from a Population Census held in 1960 and a National Household Expenditure Survey undertaken in 1961–62, in 1962 the Central Bureau of Statistics introduced a number of improvements in the methods of estimation of Gross Domestic Product and published a revised series for the years 1955–61. The data for the period 1957–62 shown in appendix table I are these revised estimates of expenditure on the Gross Domestic Product.

4 This narrow concept of current account deficit used by the Central Bureau of Statistics in estimating the GDP excludes: a) imports of ships and aircrafts, b) net transfer payments, and c) net factor income from abroad. The exclusion

tracting excess of imports over exports (item II) from gross domestic investment (item III *plus* item IV), and, thus, include both government and non-government savings.

The next stage is to solve the somewhat intricate problem of breaking these figures for total gross domestic savings and investment according to sectors. As has been already pointed out, the Central Bureau of Statistics does not publish breakdowns of gross domestic savings and investment by sectors. Our task of sectoral breakdown is made difficult by the fact that in Ghana there is no uniform concept of either the government sector or the public sector. Since a system of consolidated public sector accounts is yet to be established, the various data processing and publishing agencies in Ghana use markedly different concepts and denominations to distinguish between the public and private sectors[5]. Thus, for instance, for the purpose of national accounts, the Central Bureau of Statistics denotes consumption expenditures incurred by the Central Government, the local governments, some of the autonomous agencies and certain categories of public corporations as 'General Government Consumption Expenditure', while consumption outlays of a number of autonomous agencies and public enterprises are treated as part of 'Private Consumption Expenditure'. As compared to this classification, the budgetary data on current and capital expenditures consist of the Central Government's direct outlays on goods and services as well as its transfers to the local governments and certain categories of public institutions and statutory corporations and to the private sector, but exclude expenditures directly financed (out of current income and/or borrowing) by certain categories of public institutions and statutory corporations as well as outlays of certain public utilities such as the Ghana Railway and Ports Administration (which budgets separately) and public corporations such as the Cocoa Marketing Board. The Bank of Ghana compiles and publishes monetary data on the basis of yet another classification of the sectors: in the Bank of Ghana annual reports data on bank lending are classified into: (a) 'credit to the Government', i.e., to the Central Government, (b) 'credit to the public', i.e., to the private sector, public institutions and state enterprises, and, (c) 'credit to the Cocoa Marketing Board', i.e., cocoa financing[6].

---

of ships and aircrafts from the figures for expenditure on imports explains why in respect of certain years the data on excess of imports over exports used here differ from the figures of trade deficit shown in the official balance of payments statement (appendix table V). Although the normative significance of the definition of current account deficit used here is debatable, yet for the sake of consistency we have adhered to it.

5 The task of an analyst is further complicated by the fact that in their publications the different agencies very often do not make explicit statements about their classification of sectors and method of computation of data.

6 For further details, *see,* appendix A.

Table 13. Sources and Uses of Investment Funds, 1958–65

(In Current Prices)

(£G million)

	1958	1959	1960	1961	1962	1963	1964	1965
Sources:								
I. Gross domestic savings	69.0	81.0	83.0	54.0	71.0	77.0	105.0	74.0
1. Government sector	33.9	34.6	31.8	26.6	34.4	37.4	39.8	70.8
2. Non-government sector	35.1	46.4	51.2	27.4	36.6	39.6	65.2	3.2
II. Excess of imports of goods and non-factor services over exports of goods and non-factor services (– = Excess of exports)	–15.0	6.0	25.0	41.0	15.0	28.0	18.0	62.0
Total Sources (I + II)	54.0	87.0	108.0	95.0	86.0	105.0	123.0	136.0
Uses:								
III. Gross domestic fixed investment	55.0	77.0	97.0	105.0	92.0	109.0	116.0	135.5
1. Government sector	11.7	20.8	37.7	55.0	54.7	56.9	77.3	87.4
a) Budgeted investment	11.7	20.8	25.9	43.6	42.3	45.4	60.9	69.9
i) Direct investment	8.6	14.2	20.3	33.4	30.5	27.8	38.6	49.8
ii) Transfers to domestic sectors	3.1	6.6	5.6	10.2	11.8	17.6	22.3	20.1
b) Non-budgeted investment	–	–	11.8	11.4	12.4	11.5	16.4	17.5
2. Non-government sector	43.3	56.2	59.3	50.0	37.3	52.1	38.7	48.1
IV. Increase in stocks (– = decrease)	–1.0	10.0	11.0	–10.0	–6.0	–4.0	7.0	0.5
Total Uses (III + IV)	54.0	87.0	108.0	95.0	86.0	105.0	123.0	136.0

This lack of conceptual uniformity in the data on national accounts, budgetary expenditures and bank lending makes it necessary for us not only to choose our own definitions of government and non-government sectors but also to use indirect methods of arriving at sectoral breakdowns of total gross domestic savings and investment. For the purpose of the present analysis we have considered it useful to divide the economy into the following two sectors:

- the Central Government which henceforth shall be denoted as the government sector; and,
- the rest of the economy — that is, the private sector, the local governments, public institutions and statutory corporations, etc., which for the sake of brevity shall be referred to as the non-government sector.

The narrow definition of the government sector adopted here has two main advantages. First, it ensures conceptual consistency between our data on deficit financing and estimates of government savings and investment. Second, it permits us to make use of the budgetary data to arrive at the estimates of savings and investment in the government sector and thereby opens the door to a sectoral breakdown.

With the distinction between the government and non-government sectors established, we may now turn to an examination of the problems and methods of arriving at sectoral breakdowns. We shall begin with the assessment of government savings. There are two alternative ways of calculating government savings. The first is to take the difference between Central Government current revenue and current expenditure[7]. This is the budgetary concept of savings. The second alternative is to measure government savings by subtracting the Central Government's own consumption expenditure from its current revenue. This is the economic concept of savings which corresponds roughly to the concept of gross domestic savings implied in the national account statistics[8]. Notice that the budgetary data on current expenditure include the Central Government's own consumption expenditure on goods and services as well as its current transfers to both domestic and foreign sectors. Accordingly, the second concept of government savings is wider than the first. The question of choice between these two alternative definitions is a matter of conceptual relevance since in different contexts one may be

---

7 The data obtained according to this definition of government savings are shown in appendix table XIV. Note that to avoid any possible confusion we have denoted these figures as "current" savings.

8 For the purposes of computing "General Government consumption expenditure" and "Gross domestic fixed capital formation", the Central Bureau of Statistics makes certain adjustments in the budgetary data on current and capital expenditures by transferring those items from current expenditure which conceptually are investment outlays to gross domestic capital formation, and by moving certain items in capital expenditure which represent consumption to General Government consumption.

interested in either of them. It is clear, however, that for the purpose of the present analysis the second concept of government savings is more appropriate than the first one.

Our next task is to extract Central Government consumption expenditure from the budgetary data on current expenditure. This is made possible largely by the availability to us of the details of budgetary current expenditure from the worksheets of the Central Bureau of Statistics. In appendix table XI we have arranged these data according to Central Government consumption expenditure and its current transfers to the domestic sectors. Government savings (item I.1 in table 13) are then calculated by subtracting Central Government consumption expenditure from its current revenue (appendix table XIV). Non-government savings (item I.2 in table 13) are estimated as a residual item; they represent the difference between gross domestic savings and government savings, and, thus, include savings of the private sector, the local governments, statutory corporations, autonomous agencies, etc.

To assess the share of the government sector in gross domestic fixed capital formation we procured details of budgetary capital expenditure from the Central Bureau of Statistics. These data are presented in appendix table XII, sub-divided into direct investment and capital transfers to the domestic sectors. It should be observed that in table 13 we treat these capital transfers as part of government investment. In our view this wider concept of government investment is necessary because it permits a more consistent and meaningful assessment of the Government's contribution to the total gross domestic fixed investment.

On the uses side, a further difficulty arises from the fact that whereas the budgetary data on capital expenditure do not cover investments financed by suppliers' credits (including drawings on commercial loans in respect of Akosombo Dam)[9], machinery and equipment imported under these credit arrangements are included in the figures for gross domestic fixed capital formation[10]. To meet this gap in the budgetary data, it is necessary to make a distinction between the Government's budgeted and non-budgeted investments. While the figures for budgeted investment are taken from appendix table XII, the data on non-budgeted investment correspond to the official estimates of net suppliers' credits shown in appendix table V[11]. Non-govern-

---

9 For further details, see, appendix B.

10 In Ghana, data on gross fixed capital formation are based on imports of machinery, equipment and building materials, supplemented by estimates of non-permanent constructions, buildings and earthwork. Investments in the subsistence sector (e.g. land clearance) and cocoa planting are covered only partially. Cf. BIRMINGHAM, NEUSTADT, OMABOE (eds.), op. cit., pp. 39 and 47.

11 One important limitation of the data on suppliers' credits used here may be noted. There is considerable doubt as to the accuracy of figures for suppliers' credits. This is explained by the fact that during the period under review a

98

ment gross domestic fixed investment, item II.2 in table 13, is calculated as a residual and, thus, includes private investment as well as investments by the public corporations and public institutions, the local governments and the autonomous agencies financed from sources other than capital transfers by the Central Government. This wider definition of non-government investment is considered to be legitimate on the ground that, although most of the state enterprises, statutory corporations and public institutions depended exclusively on budgetary transfers to cover their operating losses as well as new fixed investments, some of them were able to meet their additional fixed capital requirements, at least in part, either from their operating surplus and/or by borrowing from the banking system (including the Bank of Ghana). Estimates of such 'self-financed' investments by these state enterprises and public corporations are not available. Moreover, even though separate data on bank lending to public institutions and state enterprises are available[12], the extent to which these loans were used for investment purposes is anybody's guess. The lack of precise figures notwithstanding, there are strong indications to suggest that during the period under review such 'independent' investments by the state enterprises, statutory corporations and public institutions were on the whole rather small. This means that the figures for non-government investment can be treated as rough indicators of investment activity in the private sector.

---

number of government agencies entered into such credit agreements without appropriate authorization and, what is even worse, without disclosing their commitments to a central authority such as the Bank of Ghana or the Ministry of Finance. Although since the coup in February, 1966, a number of attempts have been made to establish the exact magnitude of Ghana's obligations in respect of such credits, it would be wrong to consider the latest figures for suppliers' credits as precise and final. Yet in the context of the present analysis, the lack of precise data on total commitments does not matter much, since we are here concerned not with what Ghana owes to the rest of the world but with the extent to which such credit facilities were actually utilized for investment purposes. In other words, what matters for the purpose of the present analysis is not the total forward credit commitments which Ghana entered into during the period under review but the estimates of machinery and equipment actually received and installed under the suppliers' credits agreements. Absence of precise figures regarding the amount of such credits actually utilized in particular years is therefore a more serious aspect of the inadequacy of data on suppliers' credits.

Notice that the data on suppliers' credits used here correspond to the net value of promissory notes held by the Bank of Ghana in respect of such credits. Since some of the promissory notes are supposed to have been discounted abroad, the Bank of Ghana figures do not represent the full amount of suppliers' credit utilization. Our figures for non-budgeted investment are therefore unavoidably rough and should be so treated.

12 *See*, appendix B. Note that in order to keep our analysis conceptually consistent, we have excluded these loans from our estimates of deficit financing.

Table 14. Gross Domestic Fixed Investment at 1960 Constant Prices, 1958–65
(£G million)

	1958	1959	1960	1961	1962	1963	1964	1965
I. Gross domestic fixed Investment	58.0	82.0	97.0	100.0	91.0	108.0	110.5	125.0
1. Government sector	12.3	22.1	37.7	52.4	54.1	56.3	73.6	80.6
2. Non-Government sector	45.7	59.9	59.3	47.6	36.9	51.7	36.9	44.4
II. Increase in stocks (− = decrease)	−1.0	10.0	11.0	−10.0	−5.0	−4.0	13.0	−4.5
III. Gross Domestic Investment (I + II)	57.0	92.0	108.0	90.0	86.0	104.0	123.5	120.5

2. Estimates of Real Capital Formation

The indirect method used here for the measurement of saving and investment flows and their classification by sectors is obviously crude and debatable. However, in the absence of more detailed and precise national accounts, it offers a practical basis for extracting useful data from the available information. And despite inherent shortcomings and incomplete coverage in certain respects, the saving and investment accounts as presented here can be helpful in drawing broad conclusions on the trends in the real investment in the Ghanaian economy during 1958–65. But first we have to adjust our data on gross domestic capital formation for movements of prices. The assessment of total domestic investment in real terms, that is at constant prices, presents no difficulty since the Central Bureau of Statistics has in recent years compiled and released national income statistics also at 1960 constant prices. The data on gross domestic fixed investment and changes in stocks as given in table 14 have been taken directly from the lower half of appendix table I. As before, the main problem arises with regard to the sectoral breakdown of the aggregate gross domestic fixed investment. Since we have already computed figures for government and non-government fixed investment in current prices, the remaining task is to convert these figures to 1960 prices. To this end, we need a suitable price index for gross domestic fixed investment. This has been computed by dividing the figures of aggregate gross domestic fixed investment in current prices by their respective values at 1960 prices and multiplying the quotient by 100[13]. The figures for government and non-government gross fixed investment as given in table 13 are then deflated by this price index to arrive at their values in real terms, which are shown in table 14.

3. Level and Composition of Real Capital Formation

Table 14 shows that the real gross capital formation increased from £G149 million during 1958–59 to £G198 million during 1960–61 — a rise of 33%. In contrast, in the next two years, 1962–63, the real gross capital formation fell to £G190 million — i.e., by 4%. The reduction in the real gross investment in 1962–63 was against the background of a decreased utilization of external reserves. Whereas during 1960–61 external reserves dropped by £G93 million, in the next two-year period external reserves utilization was curtailed to £G31 million (appendix table IV). On the other hand, net inflow

---

13 The implicit price index for gross domestic fixed investment so obtained is as follows:

1958	1959	1960	1961	1962	1963	1964	1965
94.8	93.9	100.0	105.0	101.1	100.9	105.0	108.4

of foreign capital (both private and official, including IMF loan) increased significantly from £G11 million in 1960–61 to £G50 million in 1962–63 (appendix table V). On this basis, external financing in 1962–63 was £G23 million less than in 1960–61. That despite a £G23 million decrease in the utilization of external reserves and foreign capital between the two periods real gross investment in 1962–63 was only £G8 million lower than in 1960–61 is explained partly by the fact that owing to the tight restrictions on consumer goods imports in the later two-year period there was a marked shift in the composition of imports from consumer goods to investment goods. As a result, even though total imports of goods and non-factor services (in current prices) fell sharply from £G311 million in 1960–61 to £G280 million in 1962–63, investment goods imports in the latter period at £G86.4 million were only £G1 million below the level in the former period [14]. Besides the virtual stability in the level of investment goods imports in money terms, another reason why real gross investment between 1960–61 and 1962–63 fell less sharply than the current value of foreign exchange utilization was that the imports price index (1960 = 100), which in 1961 had risen to 101.2, fell steadily in 1962 and 1963 to 95.7 and 93.0 respectively. Thus, allowing for the decline in import prices, the investment goods imports in real terms increased from £G86.9 million in 1960–61 to £G91.8 million in 1962–63 [15]. It is clear from the foregoing analysis that the decline in foreign exchange utilization in money terms notwithstanding, in real terms the foreign exchange resources allocated to investment increased between the two periods. This in turn means that between 1960–61 and 1962–63 the real domestic resources allocated to investment fell more sharply than the level of real gross domestic investment.

14 Reliable estimates of investment goods imports are not available and are difficult to prepare from the existing data on imports because of lack of information on the economic use of certain sub-groups of imports. As a plausible approximation we have, however, estimated investment goods imports by adding the figures of imports of construction materials, which in the official data are shown as part of raw and semi-finished materials, to those of capital equipment (including spare parts). The yearly breakdown for 1958–1965 so obtained is as follows:

(£G million)

	1958	1959	1960	1961	1962	1963	1964	1965
Capital equipment	11.8	21.2	28.1	26.7	21.3	32.2	32.4	48.3
Construction materials	8.9	13.5	14.1	18.5	14.7	18.2	20.8	24.6
Investment goods imports	20.7	34.7	42.2	45.2	36.0	50.4	53.2	72.9

15 Since no separate price index for investment goods imports is available, the real values of investment goods imports have been calculated on the basis of year-to-year changes in the overall import price index (appendix table XIII). The annual figures of investment goods imports at 1960 constant prices so obtained are as follows:

(£G million)

1958	1959	1960	1961	1962	1963	1964	1965
21.1	34.8	42.2	44.7	37.6	54.2	51.2	67.9

Admittedly our estimates of real gross domestic investment and investment goods imports in real terms are far from perfect. Still, there cannot be much doubt about the broad conclusion that despite a more than two-fold increase in the level of deficit financing between 1960–61 and 1962–63, the process of substitution of domestic resources in favour of investment as against consumption suffered a setback.

The next two-year period, 1964–65, followed a rather different pattern. In 1964–65 external reserves fell by £G45 million and net inflow of foreign capital (minus IMF repurchase) rose to £G83 million. External financing in 1964–65 was therefore £G47 million higher than in 1962–63. Imports of investment goods in current prices between the two periods showed an increase of nearly £G40 million. However, on adjusting the 1964–65 investment goods imports figure for import price increases (the import price index rose to 104 and 107.4 in 1964 and 1965 respectively), we find that import of investment goods actually showed only an increase of about £G27 million over 1962–63. In sharp contrast, real gross investment in 1964–65 rose to £G244 million, depicting an increase of £G54 million (or 28%) over the level in 1962–63. This means that the net addition to real gross investment in 1964–65 was twice as high as the increased utilization of net foreign resources for investment. Looked at in another way, between 1962–63 and 1964–65 domestic resources allocated to investment increased by £G27 million, accounting for one-half of the increase in total real gross investment.

As noted earlier, even though the level of deficit financing during 1962–63 at £G28 million was more than twice as high as in 1961–62, gross investment between the two periods showed a decrease of 4%. The disappointing behaviour of real capital formation in what were the years of considerable deficit financing in the government sector may at first appear odd. Nor does the fact that the share of real gross investment in the constant-price GDP fell from 20% in 1960–61 to 18% in 1962–63 (*see*, table 15) seem consistent with the increased tempo of development activities in the government sector in the latter two-year period. There is, however, no real inconsistency here. A closer look at table 15 helps to explain these apparently opposite trends in the level of deficit financing and tempo of development activities in the government sector, on the one hand, and the real gross capital formation, on the other. Table 15 shows that between 1960–61 and 1962–63, while the real fixed investment in the government sector did rise from about £G90 million to some £G110 million (i.e., by about 22%), this increase was more than offset by a sharp decline both in non-government fixed investment and inventories. In real terms, gross fixed investment in the non-government sector in 1962–63 showed a decline of 17% over 1960–61, with the result that the share of non-government fixed investment in the total fell from

Table 15. Use and Supply of Resources at 1960 Constant Prices, 1958—65

(Two-year Totals)

(£G million)

	1958—59		1960—61		1962—63		1964—65	
1. Consumption	705.0	*(85)*	823.0	*(85)*	847.0	*(80)*	869.0	*(79)*
a) Government sector [a]	67.1	*(8)*	80.6	*(8)*	88.7	*(8)*	109.3	*(10)*
b) Non-Government sector [b]	637.9	*(77)*	742.4	*(77)*	758.3	*(72)*	759.7	*(69)*
2. Gross fixed investment	140.0	*(17)*	197.0	*(20)*	199.0	*(19)*	235.5	*(21)*
a) Government sector	34.6	*(4)*	90.1	*(9)*	110.4	*(11)*	154.2	*(14)*
b) Non-Government sector	105.6	*(13)*	106.9	*(11)*	88.6	*(8)*	81.3	*(7)*
3. Increase in stocks (– = decrease)	9.0	*(1)*	1.0	*(–)*	–9.0	*(–1)*	8.5	*(1)*
4. Domestic Expenditure (1 + 2 + 3)	854.0	*(103)*	1,021.0	*(105)*	1,037.0	*(98)*	1,113.0	*(101)*
5. Gross Domestic Product	833.5	*(100)*	973.0	*(100)*	1,056.0	*(100)*	1,104.5	*(100)*
6. Domestic Resource Gap (– = surplus) (4–5)	20.5	*(3)*	48.0	*(5)*	–19.0	*(–2)*	8.5	*(1)*
7. Loss from terms of trade (– = gain)	–29.5		18.0		62.0		71.5	
8. Current account deficit in balance of payments at current prices [c] (– = surplus) (6 + 7)	–9.0		66.0		43.0		80.0	

N.B. Figures in brackets are % of the GDP.

[a] These figures have been arrived at by deflating the figures of the Central Government's consumption expenditure in current prices as given in appendix table XI by the following implicit price index for General Government Consumption Expenditure which has been calculated from the data shown in appendix table I:

1958	1959	1960	1961	1962	1963	1964	1965
87.5	92.9	100.0	105.8	107.0	109.5	119.4	124.2

[b] Calculated as a balancing item.

[c] Excess of imports of goods (other than ships and aircrafts) and non-factor services over exports of goods and non-factor services, i.e., excluding transfer payments and investment income. For further details, *see*, ch. III, footnote 4.

Sources: Derived from appendix tables I and XI, and table 14.

54% to 45%, and its ratio to the constant-price GDP went down from 11% to 8%.

The declining trend in non-government fixed investment continued in 1964–65. As can be seen from table 15, despite a significant increase in the level of total fixed investment between the two periods, non-government fixed investment dropped from nearly £G87 million in 1962–63 to about £G81 million in 1964–65 — a decrease of 8%. At the same time, the share of non-government fixed investment in the total fell to 35% and its ratio to the real GDP dropped to 7%.

The above analysis shows that the last four years of the six-year period under review were marked by a persistent decline in non-government investment both in absolute and relative terms. It may be recalled here that the four-year period, 1962–65, was, on the whole, also characterized by fairly large-scale deficit financing in the government sector. It is therefore tempting to conclude that during the six-year period under review there was an inverse relationship between the dose of deficit financing and the level of non-government investment. This is an important conclusion of this study which may not be easily realized and which is significant for our analysis of the rate of growth of the economy.

The foregoing conclusion that during 1962–65 the pace of investment activity in the non-government sector suffered a setback requires one minor clarification. Note that our data on fixed capital formation in the non-government sector (as shown in tables 14 and 15) represent the aggregate of private investment and 'self-financed' investment by certain categories of public institutions and corporations. However, as mentioned earlier [16], the magnitude of the latter component of non-government investment is believed to have been rather small. Hence, the declining trend in the total non-government investment during 1962–65 by and large reflects the retarding pace of investment activity in the private sector.

The downward trend in private investment during 1962–65 does at first sight appear incongruous with the mounting inflationary pressures which, as we have seen, characterized the period. Broadly speaking, an inflationary situation acts as a tonic for investment by raising profit margins as well as future expectations of rising prices. While no precise and reliable statistical information on gross or net earnings in the private sector is available, there are strong indications that on the whole profits were being maintained at a sufficiently high level. It is for instance significant that in the manufacturing sector, which is dominated by private enterprise [17], gross profits (gross value added *minus*

16 *See*, pp. 99.

17 During 1962–1965, the private sector accounted for 80 to 90% of the total gross output in current prices in the manufacturing sector. *Cf. Economic Survey*, 1966, tables 32 and 36, pp. 60 and 63.

employment costs) as a ratio of gross output increased from 38% in 1962 to 43% in 1965 [18]. It seems therefore unlikely that the decline in investment in the private sector during 1962–65 was due to any lack of profit incentives as such.

How, then, is the decline in private investment to be explained? The 1965 *Economic Survey* throws welcome light on the causes of reduction in private investment:

"In the first place, the Government was not giving business enterprises the encouragement that they needed and in some cases Government policies tended to discourage entrepreneurs from further investment in the economy. Difficulties experienced by business concerns under the operation of import licensing and exchange controls hindered private investment and pro-

---

18		1962	1963	1964	1965
a) Gross output in the manufacturing sector in current prices (£G mill.)		35.7	46.5	53.5	60.0
b) Gross value added in the manufacturing sector in current prices (£G mill.)		20.5	26.2	29.5	34.8
c) Average annual earnings per employee in the manufacturing sector (£G)		248.4	259.2	254.4	278.4
d) Recorded employment in the manufacturing sector (thousand)		27.7	31.4	34.2	32.5
e) Employment costs in the manufacturing sector (c × d) (£G mill.)		6.9	8.1	8.7	9.0
f) Gross profits (b − e) (£G mill.)		13.6	18.1	20.8	25.8
g) Gross profits as % of gross output		38.0	39.0	39.0	43.0

Sources: Economic Survey, 1962, tables 72 and 74, pp. 79 and 82.
   Economic Survey, 1963, tables 82 and 85, pp. 116 and 119.
   Economic Survey, 1964, tables 74 and 76, pp. 105 and 108.
   Economic Survey, 1965, tables 73 and 75, pp. 98 and 100.
   Economic Survey, 1966, tables 32, 34, 69 and 71, pp. 60, 61, 92 and 95.

One important limitation of the data presented here must be noted. Whereas the figures for gross output and gross value added refer to establishments engaging 30 or more persons, the data on average annual earnings, recorded employment and employment costs pertain to establishments employing more than 10 persons. In other words, items c, d and e of the table have a wider coverage than items a and b. Because of the lack of reliable information it has not been possible for us to make necessary adjustments with a view to remove the inconsistency between the two sets of figures. It should be clear, however, that due to this lack of uniformity in our data, the figures for gross profits as % of gross output are underestimates. This is because if it has been possible to exclude employment costs in respect of establishments engaging less than 30 persons, figures of gross profits both in absolute terms and as % of gross output would have been correspondingly higher.

In view of the above as well as other limitations of the data used here, the margin of error involved is anybody's guess. None the less, we believe that our figures are not likely to be wide of the mark, especially with respect to the direction of change.

106

duction. The inability to honour matured external bills seriously eroded the confidence of the business world in the economy and by the turn of the year overseas exporters were demanding unusual guarantees before shipping goods to Ghana. Matters were not also helped by unnecessary demands for Government participation in existing profitable industrial ventures. By merely expressing interest in participation by Government, uncertainties concerning the role of private investment in Ghana were increased and this prevented the inflow of private overseas capital and the reinvestment of capital by existing private enterprises." [19]

Thus, uncertainties concerning the role of private enterprise and scarcity of foreign exchange appear to have been two important factors limiting the level of investment in the private sector during 1962—65. We have explained earlier how certain policy statements by both the Convention People's Party and the Government had already in 1962 generated widespread misgivings about the future prospects of private enterprise in Ghana [20]. Fear of outright nationalization was one aspect of these apprehensions. Risk of gradual intimidation through fiscal and monetary policies was another source of distrust. While it can be readily conceded that the fear of nationalization proved completely unfounded, the fact remains that despite the repeated assurances and generous concessions it made in the subsequent years, the Government failed to regain the confidence of private enterprise, both within Ghana and without. The explanation is to be found largely in the growing inability of the private sector to obtain sufficient foreign exchange for imports of equipment, spare parts and raw materials. Even though precise data on imports by sectors are not available, there are strong indications that during 1962–65 Government's claim on foreign exchange resources witnessed a rapid increase [21]. And idea of the inadequate foreign exchange allocation to the private sector can be had from the following figures. In 1965, when for the first time a Foreign Exchange Budget was drawn-up, out of the total planned (f.o.b.) imports of capital and consumer goods worth £G143 million, only £G53.6 million or about one-third was allocated to the private sector [22]. More significant is, however, the case of private manufacturing enterprises. In 1965 private manufacturing establishments had applied for import licences worth about £G37 million. The approved allocation of foreign exchange for these enterprises was at £G15.2 million even less than half of what they had asked for [23].

It follows from what has been said above that the scarcity of foreign exchange was in all likelihood the most important single factor limiting the level of

---

19 *Economic Survey*, 1965, p. 20, para. 85.
20 *See,* ch. II.
21 *Economic Survey*, 1965, pp. 104–105.
22 *The Budget 1965* (The Foreign Exchange Budget 1965), p. 3.
23 *Ibid.,* p. 9.

private investment in 1962–65. The decline in foreign exchange allocation for private sector investment was crucial partly because the import co-efficient for investment was rising [24] and partly because the scope for substitution between domestic and imported goods in investment remained extremely limited.

4. Deficit Financing and Resource Allocation

As we mentioned earlier, the use of the instrument of deficit financing by the government is advocated mainly on the grounds that it encourages the transfer of real resources from consumption to investment. It would be therefore useful to analyse the behaviour of real consumption and investment in Ghana with a view to throwing light on the role of deficit financing in resource allocation between consumption and investment, on the one hand, and between the government and non-government sectors, on the other.

Table 15 shows that despite a marked increase of nearly 17⁰/o in its absolute level between 1958–59 and 1960–61, the share of total real consumption in the GDP remained unchanged at 85⁰/o. In the next two-year period, 1962–63, the absolute value of total real consumption increased by slightly less than 3⁰/o while its ratio to the GDP fell to 80⁰/o. Finally, in 1964–65 the rate of increase in total real consumption fell further to 2.5⁰/o and the consumption: GDP ratio dropped to 79⁰/o.

It is noteworthy that the perceptible increase in domestic consumption during 1960–61 — the first two years of deficit financing — was accompanied by a significant rise in gross domestic investment both in absolute and relative terms. This is explained by a large-scale decumulation of external assets, particularly in 1961, through which the economy was able to acquire large import surpluses, with the result that the availability of real resources (domestic expenditure) during 1960–61 increased at a higher rate than the real GDP. Thus, the cushion of external assets made it possible to ignore the impending balance of payments crisis and to let domestic consumption and investment grow apace simultaneously.

We have seen that between 1958–59 and 1960–61 the aggregate domestic consumption ratio did not show any change. No less significant is the fact that over the same period the shares of government and non-government consumption in the GDP also remained unchanged at 8⁰/o and 77⁰/o respectively. The conspicuous stability of the government and non-government consumption ratios should not, however, mislead us. The crucial fact here is that in absolute terms government and non-government consumption expenditures

24 Yearly estimates of import co-efficient for investment are as follows:

1960	1961	1962	1963	1964	1965
0.43	0.42	0.39	0.46	0.46	0.54

108

during 1960–61 were respectively 20⁰/o and 16⁰/o higher than during 1958–59. The rate of increase in non-government consumption was far in excess of both population increase and rise in per capita income and is a clear indication of large-scale dissaving by the private sector of the economy. It seems fairly clear therefore that during the first two-year period of its use the instrument of deficit financing was not at all successful in restraining consumption.

By far the most important development during 1960–61 was a significant increase in government investment. While in absolute terms government investment during 1960–61 was nearly three times as high as during 1958–59, its ratio to the GDP over the period rose from 4⁰/o to 9⁰/o. On the other hand, whereas the absolute value of private investment during 1960–61 showed only a nominal increase of 1.2⁰/o over 1958–59, its share in the real GDP dropped from 13⁰/o to 11⁰/o. Enough has already been said to indicate the dominant role of factors like fear of nationalization and exchange controls in putting a brake on private investment, particularly in 1961. It is, however, hard to deny that the process of shift in real investment resources from private to the government sector was in part also conditioned by deficit financing.

The spectacular fall in the rate of increase of aggregate consumption expenditure during 1962–63 and the accompanying drop in the total consumption ratio were against the background of stringent import controls and deteriorating terms of trade. Towards the end of 1961 external assets had fallen to a level which was found too low to permit any further large-scale running down. At the same time, mainly due to a fall in cocoa price in the world market export receipts were becoming increasingly stagnant. It was therefore considered necessary to tackle the worsening balance of payments situation from the demand side. The more effective administration of exchange controls and the use of quantitative restrictions on import made it possible to reduce the size of current account deficit at current prices from £G66 million during 1960–61 to £G43 million during 1962–63. At constant prices, however, Ghana's exports during 1962–63 exceeded imports by £G19 million as against an import surplus of £G48 million during 1960–61. The loss resulting from the terms of trade deterioration reduced the availability of real resources to a level 2⁰/o below the value of constant-price GDP.

As a result of these developments, total domestic expenditure between 1960–61 and 1962–63 showed an increase of only 1.5⁰/o as against a rise of 8.5⁰/o in the real GDP. The modest increase in the overall domestic expenditure was, however, accompanied by three significant changes in its composition. First, even though the overall consumption ratio fell from 85⁰/o during 1960–61 to 80⁰/o during 1962–63, in absolute terms total consumption expenditure between the two periods increased by approximately 3⁰/o. Aggregate gross domestic investment on the other hand fell 4⁰/o below the 1960–61 level; over the same period the aggregate investment ratio dropped from 20% to 18%. This suggests that despite the high priority on capital goods imports the factors influencing the availability of real resources operated more against investment than against consumption. Second, as can be seen from table 15, although as a percentage of the real GDP, government consumption remained unchanged between the two periods, in absolute terms it was during 1962–63 10% above the 1960–61 level. In contrast, over the same period private consumption rose only by 2% so that during 1962–63 its ratio to the GDP dropped to 72%. However, allowing for the net increase in population at a rate of 2.6 to 3% per annum, per capita real consumption during 1962–63 was 3 to 4% below the 1960–61 level. Third, the shift in investment resources from the private to the government sector, which as we have seen was already considerable during 1960–61, became more pronounced in 1962–63. As a result, not only did the share of private investment in the real GDP witness a further decrease but, what is more significant, its absolute value also dropped considerably.

It is clear, then, that the two-year period 1962–63 was characterized by a decrease in per capita consumption as well as private investment. It is also evident that in a period in which deficit finance operations really gained momentum, the Government allowed its own consumption to rise at a considerable rate. This means that insofar as deficit financing was successful in restraining the real consumption demand, it operated mainly through a reduction in private consumption. Since government consumption during the period proved inflexible, the real resources mobilized through a reduction in per capita real consumption were merely used to pay for the rising consumption demand in the government sector. Under these circumstances, the attempt by the Government to increase the level of its own real investment was successful only at the cost of a corresponding decline in private investment.

The process of resource diversion outlined above accelerated during 1964–65. Because the possibilities of an increase in domestic production remained extremely limited, the excess demand generated by deficit financing in the government sector operated largely on the balance of payments. The current account deficit (at current prices) during 1964–65 rose to £G80 million — a record figure, which was almost twice as high as the 1962–63 level. Since, however, a large part of this massive external deficit was absorbed by the net losses resulting from further terms of trade deterioration against the country, in real terms the import surplus during 1964–65 amounted to only £G8.5 million.

Within the larger availability of real resources during 1964–65 the share of aggregate consumption in the GDP fell to 79%. In absolute terms, aggregate consumption expenditure during 1964–65 was only 2.5% higher than in the previous two-year period. However, as before, this decline in the rate of growth of total consumption expenditure resulted exclusively from the suppression of private consumption. As can be seen from table 15, the absolute level of non-government consumption expenditure remained virtually unchanged between 1962–63 and 1964–65. As a result, its share in the GDP fell further to 69% during the latter two-year period. On adjusting the 1964–65 figure for population increase, we find that per capita real consumption recorded a decrease of 5 to 6% over 1962–63. In sharp contrast, the level of government consumption at £G109 million during 1964–65 was nearly 23% higher than in 1962–63. This record rate of growth of government consumption was also reflected in a marked rise in the government consumption ratio; the share of government consumption in the GDP, which until 1962–63 had remained firm at 8%, jumped to 10% during 1964–65. Contemporaneously with the increase in use of resources for government consumption, there was also a rise in the utilization of investment resources by the Government. In absolute terms, government fixed investment during 1964–65 was nearly 40% above the 1962–63 level, whereas as a percentage of the GDP it went up to 14%. As against this, private fixed investment during 1964–65 registered further setback both in absolute and relative terms. Thus, once again the Government managed to channel an increased percentage of available resources into its own consumptions; once again the burden of holding down aggregate consumption fell solely on the private sector; and consequently, once again the Government's efforts to accelerate the tempo of its own investment activity led to a fall in private investment.

5. Paradox of 'Investment Without Growth'

Our analysis has shown that despite a significant loss of momentum in private investment during 1962–65, the economy remained geared to a high rate of investment. As explained earlier, the reduction in private investment during the period was more than offset by a substantial increase in government investment with the result that total fixed investment was running at an average annual rate of £G109 million during 1962–65 as against nearly £99 million in 1960–61 and £G70 million in the pre-deficit-financing period (1958–59).

Ironically, this increase in the rate of investment was accompanied by a declining rate of growth of the economy. The available data reveal that the Gross Domestic Product in constant prices which had increased during 1958–59 at an average rate of 6.3%, showed an increase of 5.5% per annum during 1960–61. In 1962–63 the average annual rate of growth of real GDP fell further to roughly 4%. The rate of growth of real output thereafter became much slower; it fell steadily to 2.1% in 1964 and to 1.4% in 1965.

These disappointing trends in the overall rate of growth of the real GDP tell us only a part of the story of the performance of the economy during 1960–65. The results were even more frustrating in per capita terms. During 1960–62, any increase that did occur in the GDP was increasingly absorbed by a persistent rise in population. In the later half of the six-year period under review the overall rate of growth tended to fall even below the rate of increase in population. Thus, real income per capita which between 1958 and 1962 had risen from a little more than £G61 to £G72.5, remained literally stagnant during the next two years. In 1965, the per capita real income was finally pulled down to £G71 (appendix table I).

It is clear then that during the six-year period 1960–65 there was a marked shift in the composition of domestic investment in favour of the government sector; that the rise in government investment was accompanied by a significant increase in the overall domestic investment ratio; that increasing domestic investment ratio generated declining rate of growth; and, that as a result, despite all the hardship which the rising investment ratio imposed upon them, the Ghanaians ended up with less than what they have had before. It is therefore appropriate to designate the six-year period under review as the epoch of 'investment without growth'[25].

How then can we explain the paradox of a declining rate of growth during the period of a rising rate and amount of investment? But before we proceed to analyse the causes for the opposite trends in the rates of increase of domestic investment and domestic output, it is necessary to remember that our estimates of investment are on gross basis, i.e., they do not make any allowance for depreciation. Due to the absence of reliable information on the rate of depreciation of capital stock it is not possible for us to arrive at any reasonably valid estimates of net domestic investment. One thing is, however, obvious: due to an appreciable rise in capital stock over the period, depreciation charges must have been substantially higher in the 'sixties than in the 'fifties. Admittedly, to the extent that depreciation charges were rising, the gross investment figures used here overrate the extent of net increase in capital stock. The rise in capital: output ratio (a decrease in productivity of capital), given the GDP, thus appears to be greater than it actually was. But our conclusion appears to remain valid that during the period under review a rising stock of capital was generating *falling* rates of increase in the GDP.

---

25 It is noteworthy that 'investment without growth' is also one of the main conclusions of STOLPER's book on the Nigerian economy, though his study relates to a somewhat earlier period (1950–61). *See,* W. F. STOLPER: *Planning without Facts – Lessons in Resource Allocation from Nigeria's Development* (particularly Ch. IV), Harvard University Press, Cambridge, Massachusetts, 1966.

Table 16. Percentage Distribution of Gross Domestic Fixed Capital Formation by Type, 1958—65

(Two-year Averages)

	1958—59	1960—61	1962—63	1964—65
Buildings and Construction	71	65	72	68
Transport equipment	12	18	11	13
Machinery and other equipment	17	17	17	19
Gross Domestic Fixed Capital Formation	100	100	100	100

Source: Economic Survey, 1967, tables 6 and 7, pp. 19–20.

One of the primary reasons why the domestic output grew at a decidedly lower rate than the capital stock is to be found in the structure of investment. Even though the absence of data relating to the sectoral distribution of investment prevents us from estimating the exact apportionment of investment resources between directly productive and indirectly productive projects, it seems reasonable to assume that the continuous increase in the share of the government sector in total investment during the period under review resulted in an undue emphasis on investment in schemes of social overhead capital which inevitably are highly capital-intensive and have particularly long gestation periods. The presumption is supported by the fact that, even though the Government's investment in manufacturing enterprises was rising over time, until the end of 1964 up to 70% of its development expenditure remained concentrated on less productive investments[26].

Another indication of the preponderance of less productive investment is furnished by the large share of buildings and construction in total domestic fixed investment. As can be seen from table 16, buildings and construction accounted for 65–72% of the total fixed investment during 1958–65. Apparently quite a large part of the investment in buildings and construction was devoted to residential construction both by the Government and the private sector. It is also quite likely that because of (a) scarcity of imported investment goods, (b) relatively low import-component of investment in housing, (c) extremely low rates of property tax on urban buildings[27], and (d) rising rental incomes, residential construction accounted for a much greater proportion of private investment in the later than in the earlier years. This suggests that the reduction in private investment in directly productive sectors during 1960–65 was even larger than the drop in total private investment.

The evidence is therefore strong that the net effect of rising investment in the government sector during 1960–65 was to shift the composition of total

26 *The Budget 1965* (1965 Budget Statement), p. 17, para. 67.
27 For further details, *see*, N. Aʜᴍᴀᴅ, *op. cit.*, p. 16.

investment towards projects with low and slow returns. It may be argued that to a certain degree this distortion of investment structure was inevitable, especially in a newly independent developing country like Ghana where large government outlays in power, transport facilities, irrigation and other public utilities are needed to open the way for rapid growth. A leading case in point here is the Volta River Project which absorbed nearly £G60 million before yielding the first kilowatt of electricity. While the significance of this and certain other projects of social overhead capital (e.g. Tema Harbour) cannot be challenged, it would be wrong to deny that in case of other projects of similar nature there was no room for a more thorough and objective evaluation of the implications for the economy in terms of possible economic returns. It is, in retrospect, fairly clear that a large part of government investment in schemes of social overhead capital was very tenuously, if at all, related to any possibilities of future growth. For instance, the huge capital investments in Ghana Airways and the Black Star Line were motivated primarily by the Government's desire for projecting Ghana's image abroad. Similarly, the decisions to lock vast amounts of capital in the construction of an eleven mile long super motorway between Tema and Accra, a new airport at Tamale and huge silos for storing cocoa beans at Tema were certainly motivated by considerations other than economic viability. Also the large sum spent on the construction of a monumental State House (Job 600) at a time when the economy had already reached the brink of disaster bore hardly any relation either to the then current economic situation or to any future economic returns.

In part the disappointing results during 1960–65 were due also to the lack of serious efforts to fully exploit the potential economic returns from the past investment in the social and economic infrastructure. It is well known that government investment in the 'fifties was heavily weighted in favour of infrastructural projects, of which many had passed through the gestation period by the end of the decade. Indeed, by the beginning of the 'sixties Ghana had achieved a level of infrastructural development that compared favourably with any country in tropical Africa. No doubt up to a point further social-capital investments by the Government during 1960–65 were both necessary and useful for the strength and future growth of the economy. But then the plain matter of fact is that social-overhead investments are not an end in themselves, but the means for expanding directly productive investments. In other words, government investments in social overhead capital are likely to be counter-productive unless they are combined and followed-up by carefully selected investments in productive projects that can absorb the infrastructural facilities. It seems doubtful, however, whether in disposing new investments in the 'sixties the Government of Ghana gave enough, if any, consideration to this simple but vital interrelation between investments in infrastructure and directly productive sectors. The fact that excessive emphasis in government investment on infrastructure in 1960–65 contrasted with declining private investment suggests that the Government did not take the necessary steps to stimulate productive investment and thereby to ensure the maximum use of the then existing infrastructural facilities.

Under-utilization of capital investment was by no means limited to the infrastructural facilities. Excess capacity was perhaps even more marked in the state manufacturing sector. The drive for industrialization, which was reflected in the rapid build-up of the state manufacturing sector, was motivated by the Government's desire for reducing the overwhelming dependence of the country's economy on agriculture and foreign trade. It must be admitted that in a country where agriculture accounts for about 60% of the GDP and nearly 80% of the total exports, provides a significant part of revenue to the Government and employs 60% of the total working population, industrialization was necessary not only to break the vicious circle of underdevelopment but also to diversify the production structure. It must also be recognized that in a country which is so heavily dependent on a single primary product (cocoa) for its export earnings and whose economy is therefore so easily susceptible to expansionary/contractionary forces emanating from abroad, the Government's policy of industrialization was essential for building a more self-contained and less dependent economy. The point that deserves emphasis here is, however, that even though the objective of industrialization was *per se* a sound one and cannot but be viewed sympathetically, the Government's efforts in this direction did not prove sufficiently productive. This was in large part due to the pace and style of the Government's industrialization policy. Not only did the Government attempt to introduce the techniques of modern and large-scale production rather too quickly but, worse still, it also tended to implement projects without their orderly formulation and realistic appraisal. With its increasing recourse to suppliers' credits for financing investment, the Government allowed itself to be influenced more by the recommendations of the machinery and equipment pedlars than by the judgement of its own senior technical and administrative staff. In these circumstances, the pace and direction of government investment were increasingly determined by personal whim rather than by the prospects of productive results. Consequently, many of the projects turned out to be more costly than they need have been, several of them proved to be too ambitious and prestigious, and some, like the Tema Steelworks Corporation and the Marble Works Corporation, right from the very beginning gave clear enough indications of being dead weights. Most of the state-owned manufacturing enterprises incurred considerable losses year after year. In some cases the losses were simply due to inefficient and corrupt management. A more general cause for the poor performance of the state manufacturing enterprises was the low rate of utilization of the productive capacity. An idea of the idle capacity can be had from the following figures.

Of the 20 state manufacturing enterprises which were in operation in 1964, none was running to its full capacity. Only 10 were working to half or more than half of their optimum capacities. In three cases, the actual production was even less than 10% of the full capacity. In one case (the Paper Bag Division of the Paper Conversion Corporation at Takoradi) the rate of utilization was as low as 3.5%. On average the 20 state manufacturing enterprises were using only 42% of their productive capacity. According to the *Annual Plan* for 1965, this figure was expected to rise to 67% during that year[28]. There are, however, strong indications that the average rate of utilization actually achieved during 1965 was considerably below the planned target.

The under-utilization of productive capacity in the state manufacturing sector can be attributed to a number of factors. To begin with, many enterprises with efficient management and ready market for their products were starved of necessary spare parts and raw materials. It is true that due to the virtual stagnation of receipts from exports, resulting from a sharp decline in the terms of trade, foreign exchange became an increasingly important bottleneck. It is, however, difficult to believe that, given the level of export earnings, there was no scope for a greater allocation of foreign exchange resources for import of spare parts and raw materials. Needless to say that had a higher percentage of the given foreign exchange resources been used for importing spare parts and raw materials instead of new machinery and equipment, output could have been easily increased and the growth rate would have been considerably higher.

Another factor behind the low rate of utilization of productive capacity was the scarcity of skilled manpower. The growing demand for high-level manpower was in large part met by acquiring the services of expatriate staff either by direct recruitment or through international agencies. The rapid build-up of foreign technical and supervisory personnel, though essential and beneficial, could not by itself achieve an efficient and maximum utilization of the productive capacity. At the root of the problem of under-utilization of capital was the fact that trained Ghanaian workers were not available in sufficient numbers to support the heavy investments in equipment and high-level manpower. The acute shortage of indigenous craftsmen and technicians of middle and low levels appears all the more disappointing when it is realized that during 1960–65 the Government of Ghana was devoting one-fifth to one-fourth of its current expenditures and another 8 to 10% of its capital expenditures on education and manpower training[29]. The explanation is to be found in the extremely low priority accorded to technical education

---

28 *Annual Plan for the Second Plan Year (1965 Financial Year)*, appendix 3, pp. 46–47.
29 *Cf. Economic Survey*, 1963, table VII, p. 133; *Economic Survey*, 1964, table VII, p. 120; and, *Economic Survey*, 1967, table VIII, p. 115.

and vocational training in the educational system of the country. Surprisingly enough, between 1960 and 1965, when due to the rapid expansion of the state manufacturing sector the demand for skilled workers was growing, the proportion of government educational expenditure on technical training institutes fell from 3.6% to 2.1%[30].

A final explanation for under-utilization of productive capacity in the state manufacturing sector is that, in view of the increasing centralization of decision making at the State Enterprises Secretariat, many potentially efficient and economically viable enterprises found it often difficult to obtain necessary working capital when required. The shortage of working capital became more wide-spread and serious during the final stage of the six-year period under review when, owing to the growing disparities between planned and actual expenditures — which were reflected in the frequent change of fiscal year and the increasing size of supplementary budget appropriations — the machinery for financial co-ordination and control virtually broke down.

The results of the Government's efforts in the agricultural sector were, to say the least, equally poor. The Government's strategy for agricultural development was very much similar to its industrialization strategy; namely, to acquire greater control over the sector through direct investment and to raise output through the introduction of modern methods of large-scale production. Consequently, the Government spent huge sums of money on clearing vast areas of land for cultivation, used considerable foreign exchange for the import of tractors and other items of agricultural machinery in large numbers, and employed thousands of workers to work on state farms[31]. There are clear enough indications that, as in the manufacturing sector, the results in the agricultural sector were not commensurate with the size of investment. Again as in manufacturing, the explanation is to be found in insufficient project preparation, inefficient implementation, poor management, scarcity of technical and supervisory staff and shortfalls in supplies of complementary inputs. As a result, Ghana had thousands of acres of farm land without sufficient supplies of fertilizers and high quality seeds; hundreds of tractors without adequately trained personnel to operate, maintain and repair them; tens of thousands of unskilled agricultural workers but no clear-cut policy

---

30 *Two-Year Development Plan – From Stabilization to Development (A Plan for the Period mid-1968 to mid-1970)*, July 1968, table 8.3, p. 82.

31 The management of state farms was entrusted to the following four agencies: a) the State Farms Corporation, b) the Workers' Brigade, c) the Ghana Young Farmers League, and d) the United Ghana Farmers' Co-operative Council. According to the information obtained from the Central Bureau of Statistics, at the end of 1965 the State Farms Corporation was operating 105 farms with a labour force of over 30,000, while the Workers' Brigade and the Ghana Young Farmers League had between them over 15,000 persons on pay-roll. The United Ghana Farmers' Co-operative Council which was also the sole cocoa buying agency engaged over 30,000 workers on farms and in cocoa buying.

and no effective arrangements for raising their productivity. That both physical assets and labour in the state agricultural sector were operating substantially below capacity can be seen from the fact that in 1964 the State Farms Corporation was cultivating only 3.3 acres per worker as against an acreage of 5.1 per person in small-scale peasant farming[32]. It may be argued that labour productivity in the state agricultural sector was low because a large number of state farms were in any case designed to grow new industrial crops (e.g. tobacco, rubber, cotton, sugar cane), which needed a lot of preparatory and research work before success could be assured and rapid increase in output could be achieved. This no doubt is a valid argument. But the practical question is whether, given the fact that an equally large number of state farms were used for growing food crops (rice, maize, guinea corn, groundnuts, bananas, coconuts, etc.)[33], the workers engaged on state farms were able to produce enough food for themselves? Available information suggests that they were not. It is for instance noteworthy that the rapid expansion of the state agricultural sector coincided with continuous rise in prices of locally produced foodstuffs. It is also significant that despite heavy investment in agriculture by the Government the country continued to rely heavily on imported food[34].

32 The acreage per worker was 1.5 in case of Workers' Brigade and only 0.9 for the co-operative farms managed by the United Ghana Farmers' Co-operative Council. Cf. Agricultural Census, Phase II, Vol. I, pp. 6–7. The extremely low acreage per head in the state agricultural sector demonstrates clearly that the Government's intense efforts in the agricultural sector were oriented more towards creating employment than towards raising output.

33 According to the Annual Plan for 1965, out of about 45,000 acres which the State Farms Corporation had under cultivation in 1963/64, nearly one-half was used for food crops. op. cit., p. 19.

34 See, ch. II, table 10.

Chapter IV

CONCLUSION

Over the six-year period from 1960 to 1965, with which we are concerned, deficit financing, defined to be synonymous with the increase in government net borrowing from the banking system, amounted to £G78.5 million. During the same period, the Government spent altogether £G305.2 million on capital investment and incurred budget deficits totalling £G245.9 million. On this basis, deficit financing during the period helped to finance nearly one-fourth of the government capital expenditures and as much as one-third of the budgetary deficits.

Our analysis reveals that not only the magnitude but also the impact of deficit financing varied considerably from one year to another. It is evident, however, that on the whole the level of money creation in the government sector was considerably higher in the later than in the earlier years. It is also clear that this increase in the amount of money creation over the years was not without adverse effects on both internal and external equilibrium of the economy.

The statistical evidence presented in this study shows that despite the persistent deterioration in the terms of trade after 1958, the conditions for deficit financing in the initial two years were not altogether unfavourable. The restrained resort to deficit financing by the Government during 1960–61 did not create any significant inflationary tension in the economy. In fact, the general price index (GNP deflator) in 1960 was 0.5% below its level in 1959. And, although in 1961 the price level resumed its upward trend, the rate of increase was even less than half than it had been three years earlier in 1958.

The slight drop in the general price level in 1960 and the relatively moderate rate of price inflation in 1961 were in large part due to the favourable supply conditions. Despite a significant decline since independence, the level of foreign exchange reserves at the end of 1959 was high enough to permit further drawing down in the subsequent years. The large consumer goods imports in 1960 and 1961 were a major factor in keeping the expansionary impact of deficit financing in the government sector under control. In addition, the year 1960 was marked by a significant increase in the flow of locally produced foodstuffs to the urban centres, partly due to an increase in production and partly due to improved transport facilities. And, even though domestic food production suffered a setback in 1961, due to the record high level of food imports during the year (£G26.3 million) the food situation, on the whole, remained quite satisfactory.

Another factor which tended to offset the expansionary impact of deficit financing during 1960–61 was the sharp increase in the monetary ratio (i.e., the decrease in the velocity of circulation of money). The net rise in the monetary ratio during the two-year period was of the order of 15%. Accordingly, of the total net expansion in money supply of £G14.9 million during the period, £G8.0 million — that is, more than half — was absorbed by the rise in the monetary ratio. That this increase in the monetary ratio was in large part due to certain structural changes in the economy which require additional liquidity is evident from the fact that in the next four years the monetary ratio continued to rise — albeit at a slower rate, in particular during 1962 and 1963. The persistent rise in the monetary ratio during 1960–65 supports the view that in a developing country like Ghana a considerable leeway exists for non-inflationary money creation and its use for capital formation.

The first two years of deficit financing in Ghana were also characterized by a sharp rise in the rate of real capital formation. It is noteworthy that the perceptible increase in the level of real investment during 1960–61 was not at the cost of a curtailment in per capita real consumption. Nor did the attempts by the Government to finance a part of its investment programme with created money hamper private investment activity during the period. These developments are explained by the fact that the higher domestic investment during 1960–61 was accompanied by a large-scale disinvestment in the foreign sector, which mainly took the form of a decumulation of foreign exchange reserves.

Unlike 1960–61, the last four years of the period under consideration were on the whole marked by a declining trend in both per capita real consumption and private investment. In the wake of rapidly falling external reserves a number of restrictive measures were introduced during the second half of 1961. Not only were the rates of direct and indirect taxes significantly raised, but the exchange control was also tightened. In addition, in an attempt to divert an increasing share of the foreign exchange resources to capital goods imports, the OGL was virtually suspended and the bulk of import was made subject to specific import licensing. These measures had their full impact in 1962 when, on the one hand, they led to a drastic reduction in the import of consumer goods and raw materials, and, on the other, sharply curtailed disposable private income. As a result, the year saw a sharp reduction in private consumption and investment demand. The process of the curtailment of private consumption became intensified during the subsequent three years when import restrictions became more and more stringent and taxation potential was rigorously exploited. In real terms the share of non-government consumption fell from 77% of the GDP in 1960–61 to 69% in 1964–65. This implies an annual rate of increase of only 0.5% compared with the population growth of nearly 3% per year. It is estimated that per capita real consumption fell from nearly £G56 per year during 1960–61 to about £G51 per year during 1964–65.

The contractionary impact of import and foreign exchange restrictions on private investment in 1962 was reinforced by a gradual worsening of business expectations due to political and economic uncertainties. On both these grounds, private fixed investment (in real terms) fell by more than 20% between 1961 and 1962. The notable recovery in 1963 was followed by an equally striking fall in 1964 and relative stagnation in 1965. Our estimates show that the volume of private investment during 1964–65 was nearly 25% lower than it had been during 1960–61. It seems that the sharp decline in private investment during 1962–65 was not due to any lack of profit incentives, but rather to the scarcity of foreign exchange. Though precise figures for the utilization of foreign exchange resources by sectors are not available, there are strong indications that over the years the quantitative restrictions on imports and exchange control were increasingly used as tools for distributing the scarce foreign exchange resources in favour of the government sector as against the private sector. The scarcity of foreign exchange tended to limit private investment activity partly because the import-coefficient of investment was high and partly because the scope for substitution between domestic and foreign goods in investment was extremely narrow.

While per capita consumption and private investment were falling, government consumption and investment expenditures, in particular the latter, continued to rise rapidly during 1962–65. In real terms government consumption increased at an average annual rate of about 8% between 1960–61 and 1962–65. The average rate of increase in government fixed investment over the same period was around 15% per year. Since the expansionary impact of rapid increase in government expenditure was only partly offset by the recession in private demand, aggregate demand kept rising to higher levels. On the other hand, the aggregate supply position deteriorated year after year, partly because increasing scarcity of imports of raw materials and spare parts impeded domestic production and partly because owing to the weak balance of payments position imports of consumer goods including food were drastically reduced. Unsatisfied demand spilled over into price inflation, which became particularly pronounced during 1964–65.

There is no doubt that between 1962 and 1965 deficit finance operations, combined with increased taxation, import restrictions and exchange control, were successful in squeezing per capita real consumption. But there is equally no doubt that a significant portion of the additional real resources thus mobilized by the Government was absorbed by the rapid growth of government consumption expenditure. Thus the net diversion of real resources from consumption towards investment during the period was probably not very large. It has not been possible to estimate precisely the magnitude of gross domestic savings in real terms. But there are clear indications of a declining rate of real domestic savings between 1962 and 1965. It is, for instance, significant that the ratio of gross domestic savings (in money terms) to the GDP in current prices fell from 13.9% during 1960–61 to 12.8% during 1962–63 and to 12.3 % during 1964–65. It is also noteworthy that a substantial portion of higher government investment during 1964–65 was financed by public borrowing from abroad, which took the form mainly of medium term suppliers' credits and led to a rapid build up of external debt.

Our analysis shows that total real investment (fixed), which in the two pre-deficit-financing years (1958–59) was running at an average annual rate of £G70 million, increased to £G99 million per year during 1960–61 and to £G109 million per annum during the succeeding four years. Yet despite this rapid increase in the volume of total real investment, from 1960 onwards the economy became increasingly stagnant. The real gross domestic product, which had increased at an annual average rate of more than 6% during 1958–59, rose by only 5.5% per year on average during 1960–61. During the two succeeding years the rate of growth fell to 4% per annum. The stagnation became more pronounced in 1964 and 1965 when the rate of growth in output fell far below the rate of increase in population.

A declining rate of growth during a period of rapidly rising investment turns out to be the most striking feature of Ghana's experience with deficit financing. In the final analysis, the failure of the economy to produce results commensurate with the rising level of real capital formation must be attributed to the change in the structure of investment. Over the six years from 1960 to 1965, the composition of investment shifted significantly in favour of the government sector. In fact, the rapid growth in investment after 1961 resulted solely from increased investment by the Government. It may be argued that this shift in the composition of investment was itself a policy objective. It is, however, clear that the increased utilization of investment resources by the Government was not conducive to the growth of production. The continuous rise in the share of government sector in total investment resulted in an undue emphasis on investment in schemes of social overhead capital which are highly capital-intensive and have particularly long gestation periods. In addition, increasing scarcity of imports of capital goods, spare parts and certain raw materials probably led to a sharp increase in the share of residential construction and speculative trade within the declining volume of private investment. Available information shows that the modest growth in output that took place during 1960–65 was due largely to a rise in production in certain areas within the private sector such as cocoa farming, fishing, poultry raising and internal trade, which are run primarily on traditional lines and on small scales and which, therefore, did not derive much benefit from increased government investment over the period.

The Ghanaian experience with deficit financing during 1960–65 sheds useful light on the issue as to whether, and under what circumstances, money creation by the Government can accelerate the process of economic growth in a developing country. Two important lessons can be learnt from the Ghanaian experience. The first of these relates to the crucial role of foreign exchange availabilities in deficit-financed investment programmes. The Ghanaian experience demonstrates that in a developing country where the import-content of consumption, production and investment is high, the excess demand forces generated by the deficit finance operations inevitably exert strong pressures on the balance of payments. The balance of payments difficulties would become all the more serious if, as was the case in Ghana during 1960–65, the Government's efforts to accelerate the rate of real capital formation through money creation coincide with a persistent deterioration in the terms of trade. The resort to deficit financing therefore generally necessitates both quantitative restrictions on consumer goods imports and exchange control. Admittedly these corrective measures, combined with increased tariffs and other tax restraints, can be helpful in both relieving the pressure on the balance of payments and allocating a greater share of available foreign exchange resources for investment. It must be emphasized, however, that in view of the structural characteristics of a developing country (relative inelasticity of domestic production, difficulties of producing domestic substitutes for imported consumer goods, strong preferences for imported consumer goods), it is not easy to suppress the demand for imported consumer goods beyond a certain limit. Our analysis has shown that in Ghana over the better part of the period under review the real consumption demand for imported goods continued to make significant claims on the scarce foreign exchange resources despite fairly stringent import restrictions and exchange control. The efficacy of the restrictive measures was circumvented partly by the over-riding need for imported food and partly by the failure of the Government to restrain its own consumption. Meanwhile, foreign exchange receipts from exports became virtually stagnant, despite a very large increase in volume, owing to the persistent decline in world price of cocoa (from the post-Korean peak of £G352 per ton in 1958 to £G85 per ton by July 1965). The combination of the stagnant export receipts and the relative inflexibility of consumption demand for imports tended to limit the country's capacity to import capital goods without running a current account deficit in the balance of payments. Thus, in the period in which the Government was making intensive efforts to obtain additional resources for investment through created money, the foreign exchange was becoming an increasingly crucial bottleneck. It is true that despite the adverse developments in the foreign sector and the extremely weak payments position the Government was successful in keeping the economy geared to a high rate of investment. But the crucial fact is that this success was attained at the heavy price of exhausion of large external reserves and accumulation of a huge external debt. There can be little doubt that had the large external reserves not been available and the foreign loans not been attainable, the mounting current account deficits could not have been feasible and the scarcity of capital goods imports would have seriously impeded the success of deficit-financed investment programmes.

The second lesson from the Ghanaian experience is that it is not merely the size but rather the quality of investment that determines the rate of growth of an economy. We have seen that in Ghana during the period under review increasing quantity of investment produced declining rate of growth. Our analysis has also indicated that the decrease in the productivity of investment was mainly attributable to the government sector. In fact, after 1962 not only did the preponderance of government investment lead to a sharp curtailment of private investment activity, but it also proved to be far less productive than the private investment foregone. It may be argued, with some justification, that in a young developing country investment efforts by the government cannot be exclusively growth-oriented. And, it is only fair to remember that during 1960–65 a good bit of the new investment by the Ghana Government was motivated by the desire for building a more independent and diversified economy, and for providing employment. This said, however, the fact remains that many of the government investments turned out to be more costly and less productive than they need have been. In retrospect it is clear that if government investment projects had been rationally conceived, orderly formulated, carefully implemented and efficiently managed, and if more foreign exchange had been allocated for the import of raw materials and spare parts, even a smaller quantity of investment could have yielded much better results.

APPENDICES

A. Note on Monetary Data

B. Note on Balance of Payments Data

C. List of Appendix Tables

APPENDIX A

Note on Monetary Data

The Bank of Ghana has the sole responsibility for compiling monetary data in Ghana. Monetary data are published by the Bank of Ghana in its annual reports, the *Bank of Ghana Reports,* and the *Quarterly Economic Bulletins* issued by its Research Department. As a source of basic monetary data the latter publication is, however, only marginally useful; it frequently lags behind its schedule of publication, and seldom includes any additional useful monetary statistics.

The annual reports, on the other hand, though published regularly and fairly on time since 1960[1], suffer from the lack of uniformity in the coverage and presentation of data. Furthermore, monetary data obtainable from these reports are not always consistent. Quite frequently, different issues of the annual reports give different figures for the same item; and what is even worse, at times different tables in the same issue show markedly different figures for the same item. The explanation for some of these inconsistencies is difficult to find. In many such cases, it became necessary for us to apply discretion. In few cases, a closer examination of the inconsistent figures revealed the use of different concepts. Anomalies of this nature were corrected through the time-consuming process of verification and recalculation. In this exercise, occasionally it was also found necessary to make use of the monetary data published by the Central Bureau of Statistics in the annual *Economic Surveys,* the *Statistical Year Books,* and the *Quarterly Digest of Statistics*[2].

Another serious difficulty arose out of the fact that the official publications include only rudimental monetary data for the years 1959, 1960 and 1961. Attempts to dig out certain details (for example, end of the months figures for

1 Annual reports for the financial years 1957/58 and 1958/59 were issued in mimeographed form. However, being extremely limited in scope, they offer hardly any useful data not published in the subsequent reports.
2 The monetary data published by the Central Bureau of Statistics are apparently provided by the Bank of Ghana. Nevertheless, quite often the monetary data published by the Central Bureau of Statistics differ considerably from the figures given in the Bank of Ghana publications. These obvious inconsistencies are difficult to explain.

money supply, bank lending to the government and non-government sectors and less-liquid deposits with the commercial banks) from the worksheets of the Bank of Ghana were only partially successful. The worksheets of the Bank of Ghana for the period before 1961 have not yet been fully revised and re-arranged to conform to the published data available for the ensuing years. These gaps in the published monetary data made the task of calculating the annual averages for figures of certain items for the years 1959 and 1960 rather irksome.

Finally, mention must be made of the frequent and serious printing mistakes encountered in the Bank of Ghana annual reports and the *Economic Surveys*. Since some of these mistakes repeat themselves in the subsequent issues their detection and correction demand time and patience.

Net gold and convertible foreign assets

The figures for net gold and foreign assets of the Bank of Ghana for 1965 given in tables 9 (p. 45) and 14 (p. 51) of the *Bank of Ghana Report*, June 1967, differ considerably from one another. According to the former table, at the end of 1965 the net balance of foreign exchange with the Bank of Ghana stood at £G0.3 million, but according to the latter table at £G15.6 million. It has been difficult to find any reasonable explanation for this gross discrepancy. The data on net gold and foreign assets of the Bank of Ghana used in this study (text table 3 and appendix tables IV and V) are taken from the former table since they conform to the less disputed figures for the money supply and bank lending to the government and non-government sectors.

Government indebtedness to the banking system

The figures for government borrowing from the Bank of Ghana and the commercial banks in 1963, 1964 and 1965 as shown in the *Bank of Ghana Report*, June 1967, table 9, were found to be different from those published in the earlier reports (*cf. Bank of Ghana Report*, June 1965, table XLII, and *Bank of Ghana Report*, June 1966, table 10).

On closer examination, it was discovered that these differences were due to the use of two different concepts. While in the earlier reports, government indebtedness to the banking system was calculated by subtracting "govern-ment deposits" as well as "capital accounts" from the sum of "gross current credit" and "long-term credit and securities", the data on bank credit to the Government for the years 1963, 1964 and 1965 shown in the 1967 report represent the difference between the sum of "gross current credit" and "long-term credit and securities" and "government deposits" only (i.e., the figures given in the 1967 report are *gross* of government "capital accounts", while the figures published in the earlier reports are *net* of government "capital accounts".

This change in the concept of net bank credit to the Government would not have mattered much had the new concept been explicitly stated in the 1967 report. Unfortunately, however, the 1967 report does not mention this sudden change of concept. Nor have the relevant figures for the years 1961 and 1962 been revised with the result that in the 1967 report the old and the new concepts of net bank lending to the Government are found rubbing shoulders with one another.

The figures for the Government's net indebtedness to the banking system used in this study (text table 3 and appendix table VII) are based on the new concepts. The data for the years 1959 to 1962 have been revised to conform to the new concept.

Capital and other accounts

Traditionally this item is supposed to consist primarily of capital and reserve funds of the banking system. A closer look at the published data on this item, however, raises serious doubts about its exact composition. The 1967 report, for instance, shows large negative figures under this item for the years 1963, 1964 and 1965 (£G0.2 million, £G14.8 million, and £G20.9 million respectively) and thereby suggests significant year-to-year deteriorations in the "capital and other accounts" of the banking system from 1962 onwards. The explanation for this development is, however, hard to find. The annual reports of the Bank of Ghana do not go into details of composition and method of computation of this item. The brief references to the changes in "capital and other accounts of the banking system" found here and there in the annual reports are not helpful in opening the door to the possible adjustments and improvements in the published data.

Although the authenticity of the data on this item for the years 1963, 1964 and 1965 seems doubtful, the lack of explicit details has prevented us from attempting any meaningful revision and readjustment. The figures for this item used in the present study (text table 3 and appendix table VI) are therefore primarily taken from the annual reports. The data for the period from 1959 to 1962 have been, however, adjusted for the exclusion of government "capital accounts" from our estimates of net bank lending to the Government.

Bank lending to the non-government sector

This item covers lending by the Bank of Ghana and the commercial banks to:

• the private sector;
• the state enterprises and autonomous agencies such as the Ghana Railway and Ports Administration; and,
• the Ghana Cocoa Marketing Board (for cocoa financing).

The official publications are not consistent in the denomination of bank credit to these sectors of the economy. Till very recently, bank lending to these sectors was frequently dubbed either "credit to the private sector" or "credit to the public". This is one of the reasons why separate figures for bank credit to the private sector, the state enterprises and public institutions, and the Cocoa Marketing Board were until recently not readily available. In the *Bank of Ghana Report*, June 1967, these vague and somewhat misleading titles were replaced by a more appropriate and explicit designation, viz. "bank lending to the public institutions and private sector".

The data on this item (text table 3 and appendix tables VIII and IX), which in this study is denoted as "bank lending to the non-government sector", are taken from the consolidated balance sheets of the banking system published in the various issues of the Bank of Ghana annual reports.

Separate figures for gross bank lending to the private sector, the state enterprises and public institutions, and the Cocoa Marketing Board are available from 1961 onwards and are shown in the following table.

Gross Bank Lending to the Non-Government Sector
(At the End of Year)
(£G million)

Year		Private Sector	Public Institutions and State Enterprises	Cocoa Marketing Board [a]	Total Gross Lending [b]
1961	Bank of Ghana	–	–	–	–
	Commercial Banks	26.8 [c]	–	0.4	27.2
1962	Bank of Ghana	–	–	–	–
	Commercial Banks	20.0 [c]	–	10.5	30.5
1963	Bank of Ghana	–	–	14.5	14.5
	Commercial Banks	17.9	8.0	15.9	41.8
1964	Bank of Ghana	–	1.2	32.0	33.2
	Commercial Banks	16.0	9.8	17.3	43.1
1965	Bank of Ghana	–	0.3	22.0	22.3
	Commercial Banks	25.4	17.2	20.0	62.6

[a] Excluding credits against foreign securities pledged with the Bank of Ghana in 1961 (£G20 million) and 1962 (£G 23.7 million). From the view point of overall monetary expansion these exclusions do not matter much, since these transactions are reflected in our data on foreign reserves of the Bank of Ghana.
[b] Without deducting increase in time and savings deposits and advance deposits against import licenses.
[c] Including credits to the public institutions and state enterprises. Breakdown is not available.

Sources: *Economic Survey*, 1967, tables XXII and XXIII, pp. 133–134, and direct information from the Bank of Ghana.

APPENDIX B:

Note on Balance of Payments Data

The balance of payments data presented in appendix table V have been derived mainly from the official balance of payments statements published in the series of *Economic Surveys, Bank of Ghana Reports* and *Statistical Year Books*.

In recent years the balance of payments statistics have undergone a series of changes both in respect of classification and coverage, especially of capital account data. Largely as a result of frequent revisions, but partly also due to printing errors (which in certain cases have been carried over year after year), balance of payments statistics obtainable from various official publications display discrepancies and inconsistencies. It has therefore been found necessary to cross-check balance of payments data from various official publications, and select the latest figures available. In addition, to the extent possible, an attempt has been made to reclassify some of the items pertaining to the earlier years in the series with a view to make them conform with the definitions and concepts of estimation introduced in recent years. It may, however, be noted that these attempts notwithstanding, the capital account data for the years 1958 to 1962 suffer from incomplete coverage, especially in respect of suppliers' credits, private investment, trade credits, etc., and should therefore be considered rough indicators.

The concepts used in the estimation of the following items need some explanation.

1. Non-factor services (item 4) represent the difference mainly between:
    a) foreign exchange receipts of the Black Star Line and the Ghana Airways *plus* local expenses of foreign airlines and shipping companies *plus* non-merchandise insurance, postal settlements, etc. *plus* local expenses of foreign diplomatic missions; and,
    b) payments to foreign shipping firms and airlines in respect of merchandise freight and insurance *plus* private and business travel expenditure *plus* students' expenditure *plus* expenses of Ghana's diplomatic missions abroad *plus* non-merchandise insurance *plus*

contributions to head office expenses abroad by Ghana branches of foreign companies *plus* film rentals, commissions, etc.

2. Investment income (item 5) represents the difference mainly between the estimates of profits of foreign investment in Ghana and the earnings from foreign securities held by the Bank of Ghana. Since 1963 this item also covers estimates of interest payable on utilized suppliers' credits.

3. Transfer payments (item 7) cover:
(on the receipts side) imports of cars and other consumer goods involving no remittance of foreign exchange, remittances from Ghanaians working abroad, gifts and transfer of legacies, grants and subventions by international organisations and foreign governments, and imports under the World Food Programme.
(on the payments side) remittances by foreign workers (which up to 1962 were included under travel), payments of retirement compensation to foreigners giving up residence in Ghana, contributions to international agencies and the African Development Bank.

4. Decrease in external assets of the bank and the non-bank sectors (items 9a and 9b) shows the net change in international reserves excluding drawings on the IMF and bilateral trade balances. For some reason (time-lag in recording foreign liabilities? use of slightly different concepts?), the figures on these items obtainable from the official balance of payments statements vary, in some cases considerably, from the data published elsewhere in the Bank of Ghana annual reports. For the sake of consistency, the figures on external assets have been derived from appendix table IV rather than from the official balance of payments statements.

5. Government long-term loans (item 10a) cover long-term credits to certain African countries:
1959: £G4 million to Guinea;
1961: £G5 million to Mali;
  £G4 million to Upper Volta, of which £G2 million represented advance re-imbursement of import duties on goods of non-Ghanaian origin bought by Upper Volta;
  £G1 million to Guinea (balance of previously granted loan)[1].

6. Government capital investment (item 10b) in 1961 represents the purchase of certain foreign-owned gold mines by the Government.

---

1 According to the Auditor-General's Report, the loan to Guinea is not covered by any formal agreement, while the agreements relating to loans to Mali and Upper Volta are yet to be ratified. Guinea has not so far made any repayment on the principal. Repayments of loans to Upper Volta and Mali were not due to begin until 1967. *See, Report and Financial Statements by the Accountant-General and Report thereon by the Auditor-General for the period ended 31st December, 1964*, Accra, 1967, p. 7.

131

7. Suppliers' credits (item 10c) are relatively medium-term loans obtained by the Government from foreign official and private sources for financing specific projects. This item also includes commercial credits from lending agencies in respect of Volta River Project (1962 = £G0.1 million; 1963 = £G8.1 million; 1964 = £G7.8 million; 1965 = £G7.2 million).

8. Bilateral trade balances (item 10d) represent the net position on transactions with the following countries with which Ghana concluded bilateral trade and payments agreements between 1958 and 1962:

Albania, Bulgaria, China (mainland), Cuba, Czechoslovakia, Dahomey, East Germany, Guinea, Hungary, Israel, Mali, Poland, Romania, UAR (Egypt), USSR, Upper Volta and Yugoslavia.

These agreements, particularly those with the state-trading countries, provided for the sale of Ghana products, mainly cocoa, in exchange for consumer and investment goods from bilateral trade partners. Payments under these agreements are effected through the Bank of Ghana and the central banks of the trade partner countries. Under these clearing account agreements Ghana is entitled to securing credit facilities ranging from £G30,000 to £G4 million. Balances in excess of swing credit limits are settled either through delivery of goods or through payments in convertible currency after a special protocol.

The agreement with Upper Volta was concluded in 1960 when a free trade area between Ghana and Upper Volta was established. Under this agreement goods were to move between the two countries free of duty, and duties collected on goods imported into Ghana and re-exported to Upper Volta were to be reimbursed to Upper Volta.

Also the agreement with Mali resulted from a special situation in which Ghana's persistent short-term trade deficit resulting from her meat imports is offset by a long-term loan of £G5 million from Ghana to Mali in 1961.

9. Advance financing of cocoa in 1960 and 1961 (item 10e).

The explanation for these mutually neutralizing entries is to be found in the changes in the cocoa financing system introduced in the 1960/61 and 1961/62 crop seasons.

Up to the 1959/60 season, the Cocoa Marketing Board used to finance the marketing of cocoa crop largely by using its own liquid resources, and partly by borrowing in London where its financial transactions were carried out by its subsidiary marketing company, the Ghana Cocoa Marketing Company Limited.

For a number of reasons, including the fact that the system required the maintenance of a considerable proportion of the Board's resources in cash or highly liquid assets, it was decided to replace the cash financing system by a bill finance scheme. Under the new method of cocoa financing, introduced during the 1960/61 crop season, the Board met its requirements for cash by drawing 90-days bills of exchange on its subsidiary marketing company in London. The bills of exchange were then discounted by the Board with the Ghana Commercial Bank, a government owned bank, which initially had the monopoly for handling these bills. Under the scheme, the Ghana Commercial Bank could in turn rediscount such bills with the Bank of Ghana which backed the scheme by providing rediscount facilities up to a limit arranged from time to time. The rediscounted bills were considered sterling bills and taken up by the Issue Department of the Bank of Ghana as part of the currency cover[2].

Following the introduction of the bill finance system, a large part of cocoa financing during the main crop season in 1960/61 was done by three-months bills of exchange. The positive figure of £G14 million indicated under 'advance cocoa financing' for 1960 represents the amount of cocoa bills rediscounted and held by the Bank of Ghana at the end of that year.

As indicated earlier, these bills were treated by the Bank of Ghana as short-term sterling assets. The significant rise in 1960 in the external reserves of the Bank of Ghana is attributable largely to this factor. Viewed from the opposite angle, the same factor also explains in part the considerable decrease in the external reserves of the non-bank sector, including the Cocoa Marketing Board (appendix table IV).

Further changes in the method of cocoa marketing and financing were introduced at the beginning of the 1961/62 crop season (October, 1961) when it was decided to transfer the Cocoa Marketing Company from London to Accra. In brief, the new scheme involved:

- the surrender of foreign long-term securities held by the Cocoa Marketing Board to the Bank of Ghana;
- the transfer by the Bank of Ghana to the Ghana Commercial Bank of a sum equivalent to the market value of these securities on the date of their surrender; and,
- the channelization of these funds by the Ghana Commercial Bank to the Board as and when the need arose.

The long-term foreign securities so obtained by the Bank of Ghana were used to issue currency for the purpose of cocoa financing.

The negative figure of £G14 million in 1961 merely reflects these changes in the cocoa financing system: the £G14 million-worth of cocoa bills, which under the previous system would on maturity in 1961 have led to a corresponding reduction in the Bank of Ghana's short-term external assets, were with the introduction of the new scheme settled against the

---

2 For further details, see, *Bank of Ghana Report*, June 1961, pp. 5–6.

long-term external securities surrendered by the Board to the Bank of Ghana. Looked at from the opposite side, the Bank of Ghana acquired long-term assets in exchange for its short-term holdings.

10. Trade credits (item 10f) reflect the net effect of the changes in imports and export credits. Separate data on this item are not available for the period 1958–62. Also the figure for 1963 is a rough estimate and should be so treated. The large inflow of capital on this account in 1965 resulted from the introduction of the policy making it obligatory to finance all current imports not covered by other credit arrangements by 180-days trade credits instead of by payments at sight.

11. Private investment (item 10g) includes:

- investments by foreign private firms (new capital inflow *plus* undistributed profits retained for investment in Ghana);
- investment by the Volta Aluminium Company (VALCO); 1965 = £G5.5 million; and,
- distributed profits of foreign enterprises which due to exchange control restrictions could not be repatriated. These accumulated profits are treated as 'reinvested' in the official balance of payments statements. In the absence of reliable information on the level of such unremitted profits, it has not been possible to separate them from private investment as such. In any case, it seems unlikely that this item is fully covered by the official statistics, especially for the first few years immediately after the introduction of exchange control.

12. Errors and omissions (item 11): Relatively large negative figures for 1960 and 1961 are believed to consist mainly of private capital outflows before the introduction of exchange control regulations on 1st July, 1961. The large negative figures for 1963, 1964 and 1965 reflect largely the adjustments made to this item for the discrepancies in the data on external assets actually used here and the figures given in the official balance of payments statements.

APPENDIX C

List of Appendix Tables

Table I. Expenditure on Gross National Product at Current and 1960 Constant Prices, 1957–65 (£G million)

	1957	1958	1959	1960	1961	1962	1963	1964	1965
At Current Prices									
1. Private consumption expenditure	298.0	286.0	325.0	347.0	402.0	415.0	458.0	493.5	627.5
2. General Government consumption expenditure	33.0	35.0	39.0	48.0	55.0	61.0	69.0	80.0	102.5
3. Gross domestic fixed investment	56.0	55.0	77.0	97.0	105.0	92.0	109.0	116.0	135.5
4. Increase in stocks	−6.0	−1.0	10.0	11.0	−10.0	−6.0	−4.0	7.0	0.5
5. Domestic expenditure (1 + 2 + 3 + 4)	381.0	375.0	451.0	503.0	552.0	562.0	632.0	696.5	866.0
6. Exports of goods and non-factor services	96.0	110.0	120.0	123.0	122.0	120.0	117.0	123.5	126.0
7. Imports of goods and non-factor services	107.0	95.0	126.0	148.0	163.0	135.0	145.0	141.5	188.0
8. Expenditure on gross domestic product (5 + 6 − 7)[b]	370.0	390.0	445.0	478.0	511.0	547.0	604.0	678.5	804.0
9. Net factor income from abroad[a]	−3.0	−2.0	−3.0	−5.0	−7.0	−5.0	−9.0	−6.0	−9.5
10. Expenditure on gross national product (8 + 9)	367.0	388.0	442.0	473.0	504.0	542.0	595.0	672.5	794.5
11. Rate of growth of GNP	4.6	5.7	13.9	7.0	6.6	7.5	9.8	13.1	18.1
12. Estimated Population (in millions)[c]	6.1	6.3	6.5	6.7	6.9	7.1	7.3	7.5	7.7
13. Per capita gross national product (£G)	60.1	61.6	68.0	70.5	73.0	76.5	82.0	90.0	103.5
At 1960 Constant Prices									
1. Private consumption expenditure	304.0	295.0	328.0	347.0	376.0	355.0	372.0	358.5	361.0
2. General Government consumption expenditure	40.0	40.0	42.0	48.0	52.0	57.0	63.0	67.0	82.5
3. Gross domestic fixed investment	58.0	58.0	82.0	97.0	100.0	91.0	108.0	110.5	125.0
4. Increase in stocks	−6.0	−1.0	10.0	11.0	−10.0	−5.0	−4.0	13.0	−4.5
5. Domestic expenditure (1 + 2 + 3 + 4)	396.0	392.0	462.0	503.0	518.0	498.0	539.0	549.0	564.0
6. Exports of goods and non-factor services	107.0	94.0	109.0	123.0	138.0	162.0	154.0	135.5	167.0
7. Imports of goods and non-factor services[a]	109.0	97.0	126.5	148.0	161.0	141.0	156.0	136.0	175.0
8. Expenditure on gross domestic product (5 + 6 − 7)	394.0	389.0	444.5	478.0	495.0	519.0	537.0	548.5	556.0
9. Net factor income from abroad[b]	−3.0	−2.0	−5.0	−5.0	−7.0	−5.0	−9.0	−6.0	−9.5
10. Expenditure on gross national product (8 + 9)	391.0	387.0	439.5	473.0	488.0	514.0	528.0	542.5	546.5
11. Rate of growth of GNP	2.4	−1.0	13.7	7.5	3.2	5.3	2.7	2.8	0.7
12. Per capita gross national product (£G)	64.1	61.4	67.6	70.5	71.0	72.5	72.5	72.5	71.0

[a] Excluding ships, fishing trawlers and aircrafts (except one VC-10 aircraft imported in 1965).

[b] Excluding transfer payments.

[c] Population figures for 1960–65 are derived from the data on GNP and per capita GNP given in the *Economic Survey*, 1966 (table 2, p. 12). The data for 1957–59 are rough estimates calculated on the assumption that between 1957 and 1960 the population in Ghana was growing at the rate of 3% per annum.

Sources: Economic Survey, 1964, table 2, p. 16.
Economic Survey, 1965, table I, p. 107.
Economic Survey, 1966, tables 2, 3 and I, pp. 12, 14 and 100.
Direct Information from the Central Bureau of Statistics.

Table II. Money Supply, 1959–65

Year	At the End of Year					Average of End of Month Figures				
	Currency in Active Circulation (£G '000)	Demand Deposits (£G '000)	Money Supply (£G '000)	Increase over Previous Year (— = decrease) (£G '000)	Rate of Increase (— = decrease)	Currency in Active Circulation (£G '000)	Demand Deposits (£G '000)	Money Supply (£G '000)	Increase over Previous Year (— = decrease) (£G '000)	Rate of Increase (— = decrease)
1959	37,481	19,656	57,137	—	—	27,359	20,106	47,465	—	—
1960	43,537	23,626	67,163	10,026	17.5	30,870	22,690	53,560	6,095	12.8
1961	43,247	29,744	72,991	5,828	8.5	35,620	26,690	62,310	8,750	16.3
1962	47,220	34,390	81,610	8,619	11.8	38,800	28,338	67,138	4,828	7.8
1963	48,875	37,463	86,338	4,728	5.8	39,735	35,808	75,543	8,405	12.5
1964	66,627	54,252	120,879	34,541	40.0	48,257	44,395	92,652	17,109	22.6
1965	57,917	62,333	120,250	−0,629	−0.5	57,808	56,158	113,966	21,314	23.0

Sources: Bank of Ghana Report, June 1960, appendices 2, 4 and 6, pp. 17, 19, 22 and 23.
Bank of Ghana Report, June 1961, tables 2, 5a, 6 and 8, pp. 28, 29, 32, 34, 35 and 37.
Bank of Ghana Report, June 1962, table 8, p. 45.
Bank of Ghana Report, June 1963, table XXXIX, p. 51.
Bank of Ghana Report, June 1964, table XLVIII, p. 56.
Bank of Ghana Report, June 1965, table 8, p. 105.
Bank of Ghana Report, June 1966, table 6, p. 51.
Bank of Ghana Report, June 1967, table 5, p. 41.

Table III. **Price Index (GNP Deflator), 1957—65**
(1960 = 100)

Year	GNP in Current prices (£G million) (Y)	GNP in 1960 constant prices (£G million) (X)	Price Index ($\frac{Y}{X} \times 100$)	Rate of Increase of prices (— = decrease)
1957	367	391	93.86	—
1958	388	387	100.26	6.8
1959	442	440	100.45	0.2
1960	473	473	100.00	−0.5
1961	504	488	103.28	3.3
1962	542	514	105.45	2.1
1963	595	528	112.69	6.9
1964	673	543	123.94	10.0
1965	795	547	145.34	17.3

Source: Appendix table I.

Table IV. **Net Gold and Convertible Foreign Assets** [a], **1957–65**
(£G million)

End of Year	Bank of Ghana	Commercial Banks	Total Bank Sector (1 + 2)	Decrease over previous year (— = increase)	Non-Bank Sector [b]	Decrease over previous year (— = increase)	Grand Total (3 + 5)	Decrease over previous year (4 + 6) (— = increase)
	1	2	3	4	5	6	7	8
1957	38.2	10.6	48.8	–	122.7	–	171.5	–
1958	31.1	14.4	45.5	3.3	127.6	-4.9	173.1	-1.6
1959	43.4	10.8	54.2	-8.7	112.5	15.1	166.7	6.4
1960	53.8	6.5	60.3	-6.1	88.3	24.2	148.6	18.1
1961	45.4	3.1	48.5	11.8	25.3	63.0	73.8	74.8
1962	47.9 [c]	-2.3	45.6	2.9	26.8	-1.5	72.4	1.4
1963	35.3	-6.0	29.3	16.3	14.0	12.8	43.3	29.1
1964	27.3	-3.8	23.5	5.8	7.4	6.6	30.9	12.4
1965	0.3	-8.9	-8.6	32.1	6.5	0.9	-2.1	33.0

[a] Excluding net drawings from IMF and balances resulting from bilateral payments agreements.
[b] Treasury and other official institutions including, till 1962, Cocoa Marketing Board, Local Authorities and Higher Educational Institutions. In September 1963 foreign assets of these institutions were taken over by Bank of Ghana.
[c] The increase in the reserves resulted almost exclusively from the acquisition by the Bank of Ghana foreign securities worth about £G2 million which certain enterprises held as pensions funds. These securities had before 1962 not been included in the calculation of external assets.

Sources: Economic Survey, 1964, tables XVII and XX, pp. 134 and 138. *Economic Survey*, 1965, table XIX, p. 132. *Economic Survey*, 1966, table XIX, p. 120. *Bank of Ghana Report*, June 1965, tables XLII, LIV and 9, pp. 58, 88 and 106. *Bank of Ghana Report*, June 1966, tables 10 and 15, pp. 55 and 60. *Bank of Ghana Report*, June 1967, tables 9 and 14, pp. 45 and 51.

Table V. Balance of Payments, 1958–65 (£G million)

	1958	1959	1960	1961	1962	1963	1964	1965
1. Merchandise imports (f.o.b.)	78.1	106.8	124.3	137.4	110.8	120.3	114.9	156.2
2. Exports (f.o.b.)	107.1	113.0	119.2	118.8	114.2	109.6	114.8	114.7
a) Merchandise	(96.5)	(101.8)	(108.1)	(108.2)	(102.9)	(98.3)	(104.5)	(105.2)
b) Non-monetary gold	(10.6)	(11.2)	(11.1)	(10.6)	(11.3)	(11.3)	(10.3)	(9.5)
3. Trade deficit (1–2) (– = surplus)	–29.0	–6.2	5.1	18.6	–3.4	10.7	0.1	41.5
4. Non-factor services (net)	13.0	11.5	23.3	23.1	20.9	19.0	20.4	25.6
5. Investment income (net outflow)	1.3	1.6	5.5	5.5	5.0	9.0	6.3	9.7
6. Excess of imports of goods and services over exports of goods and services (3 + 4 + 5). (– = excess of exports)	–14.7	6.9	33.9	47.2	22.5	38.7	26.8	76.8
7. Transfer payments (net)	2.5	2.2	4.8	5.5	5.7	7.0	7.9	4.7
8. Deficit on current account (6 + 7) (– = surplus)	–12.2	9.1	38.7	52.7	28.2	45.7	34.7	81.5
9. Monetary movements	–1.6	4.8	18.1	74.8	6.5	29.1	12.4	29.2
a) Decrease in external assets of the bank sector[a] (– = increase)	3.3	–8.7	–6.1	11.8	2.9	16.3	5.8	32.1
b) Decrease in external assets of the non-bank sector[a] (– = increase)	–4.9	15.1	24.2	63.0	–1.5	12.8	6.6	0.9
c) IMF loans (– = repurchases)	–	–1.6	–	–	5.1	–	–	–3.8
10. Official and private capital	–10.7	4.3	29.0	–18.1	20.9	24.4	27.7	58.7
a) Government long-term loans	–1.6	–4.0	–	–10.0	–	–	–	–
b) Government capital investment	–	–	–	–5.5	–	–	–	–
c) Suppliers' credits (net)	–	–	11.8	11.4	12.4	11.5	16.4	17.5
d) Bilateral trade balances (net)	–	–	–	–	1.7	1.8	1.5	12.4
e) Advance cocoa financing	–	–	14.0	–14.0	–	–	–	–
f) Trade credits (net)	} –9.1	} 8.3	} 3.2	} –	} 6.8	1.7	4.5	21.5
g) Private investment						9.4	5.3	7.3
11. Errors and omissions	0.1	–	–8.4	–4.0	0.8	–7.8	–5.4	–6.4

a For the sake of consistency these figures have been taken directly from appendix table IV. Since some of these figures do not agree with the data obtainable from the official balance of payments statements, adjustments have been made in certain other items where necessary.

Sources:

Statistical Year Book, 1963, table 134, pp. 138—139 (for 1958, 1959 and 1960).
Economic Survey, 1960, table 85, pp. 91—92 (for 1959).
Economic Survey, 1961, table 106, pp. 125—126 (for 1959 and 1960).
Economic Survey, 1964, tables X and XI, p. 128 (for 1961).
Economic Survey, 1965, tables XI and XII, p. 120—122 (for 1962).

Bank of Ghana Report, June 1964, table XIX, p. 25 (for 1962).
Bank of Ghana Report, June 1965, table XX, pp. 32—33 (for 1963).
Bank of Ghana Report, June 1966, table 14, p. 59 (for 1964).
Bank of Ghana Report, June 1967, table 13, p. 50 (for 1965).

N.B. For further details, *see,* appendix B.

Table VI. Monetary Developments in Ghana, 1960–65
(£G million)

	1960	1961	1962	1963	1964	1965
A. Internal Credit Monetization (1–2)	0.0	20.6	7.7	24.7	22.9	53.4
1. Increase in gross bank lending	7.0	19.0	14.8	24.5	22.1	58.2
2. Increase in domestic bank liabilities other than money (a + b)	7.0	–1.6	7.1	–0.2	–0.8	4.8
a) Increase in less-liquid deposits with the commercial banks	(1.8)	(2.2)	(2.2)	(4.4)	(7.7)	(8.4)
b) Increase in other domestic liabilities of the banking system	(5.2)	(–3.8)	(4.9)	(–4.6)	(–8.5)	(–3.6)
B. External Credit Monetization (3 + 4 + 5)	53.2	44.9	24.5	37.2	34.3	55.8
3. Decrease in net external assets of the non-bank sector (– = increase)	24.2	63.0	–1.5	12.8	6.6	0.9
4. IMF loans (– = repurchases)	–	–	5.1	–	–	–3.8
5. Increase in foreign liabilities of the non-bank sector (– = decrease)	29.0	–18.1	20.9	24.4	27.7	58.7
C. Current Credit Monetization (A + B)	53.2	65.5	32.2	61.9	57.2	109.2
D. Relative Contraction of Monetary Liquidity (6–7)	–2.7	–5.3	–0.1	–1.8	–7.2	–4.5
6. Additional monetary requirements on the basis of previous year's monetary ratio	3.4	3.5	4.7	6.6	9.9	16.8
7. Actual increase in money supply	6.1	8.8	4.8	8.4	17.1	21.3
E. Total Monetary Financing (C + D)	50.5	60.2	32.1	60.1	50.0	104.7
Absorbed by:						
F. Increase in Domestic Production	3.6	1.7	3.3	1.8	2.1	0.7
G. Increase in Internal Prices	–0.2	1.8	1.4	4.8	7.8	16.1
H. Deficit on Current Account	38.7	52.7	28.2	45.7	34.7	81.5
I. Errors and Omissions in Balance of Payments	8.4	4.0	–0.8	7.8	5.4	6.4

N.B. For an explanation of the concepts and method of calculation, *see*, appendix A.

Table VII. **Government Indebtedness to the Banking System**[a], **1959–65**

(£G million)

Year	At the End of Year				Average of End of Month Figures			
	To the Bank of Ghana	To the Commercial Banks	Total	Increase over Previous Year	To the Bank of Ghana	To the Commercial Banks	Total	Increase over Previous Year
1959	-1.3	-1.5	-2.8	–	-1.4	-1.5	-2.9	–
1960	-1.3	2.7	1.4	4.2	-1.4	2.3	0.9	3.8
1961	6.5	5.5	12.0	10.6	4.1	5.3	9.4	8.5
1962	13.3	12.9	26.2	14.2	9.9	13.4	23.3	13.9
1963	16.2	16.0	32.2	6.0	19.9	17.6	37.5	14.2
1964	28.6	35.3	63.9	31.7	17.6	25.0	42.6	5.1
1965	62.7	33.3	96.0	32.1	38.1	37.5	75.6	33.0

[a] Gross current credit *plus* long-term credit and securities *minus* government deposits.

Sources: *Bank of Ghana Report*, June 1960, appendices 1, 2 and 6, pp. 14–17 and 22–23.
Bank of Ghana Report, June 1961, table 6, pp. 34–35.
Economic Bulletin of Ghana, Vol. 3, No. 4 (April, 1959), p. 19.
Economic Bulletin of Ghana, Vol. 3, No. 5 (May, 1959), p. 24.
Statistical Year Book, 1961, table 138(a), p. 125.
Bank of Ghana Report, June 1963, table XLIII, p. 60.
Bank of Ghana Report, June 1964, tables XLV and LII, pp. 49 and 65.
Bank of Ghana Report, June 1965, tables XLII and XLIX, pp. 58 and 72.
Bank of Ghana Report, June 1967, table 9, p. 45.
Worksheets of the Research Department, Bank of Ghana.

Table VIII. Bank Lending to the Non-Government Sector, 1959–65

(£G million)

At the End of Year	By the Bank of Ghana 1	By the Commercial Banks 2	Total Gross lending [a] (1 + 2) 3	Time, Savings and other deposits with the Commercial Banks [b] 4	Net Lending (3—4) 5	Increase in net lending over previous year (— = decrease) 6
1959	—	14.8	14.8	11.3	3.5	—
1960	—	19.8	19.8	13.1	6.7	3.2
1961	—	27.2	27.2	13.7	13.5	6.8
1962	—	30.5	30.5	17.7	12.8	-0.7
1963	14.5	41.8	56.3	21.2	35.1	22.3
1964	33.1	43.1	76.2	27.8	48.4	13.3
1965	22.3	62.5	84.8	31.0	53.8	5.4

[a] Excluding credits against foreign securities pledged with the Bank of Ghana by the Cocoa Marketing Board in 1961 (£G20 million) and 1962 (£G23.7 million).
[b] Time deposits *plus* savings deposits *plus* advance deposits against imports licences.

Sources: *Bank of Ghana Report*, June 1965, tables XLII and XLVII, pp. 58 and 68.
Bank of Ghana Report, June 1967, tables 5 and 9, pp. 41 and 45.
Worksheets of the Research Department, Bank of Ghana.

Table IX. Bank Lending to the Non-Government Sector, 1959–65
(£G million)

Average of End of Month Figures	By the Bank of Ghana 1	By the Commercial Banks 2	Total Gross lending [a] (1 + 2) 3	Time, Savings and other deposits with the Commercial Banks [b] 4	Net Lending (3–4) 5	Increase in net lending over previous year (— = decrease) 6
1959	—	10.4	10.4	9.7	0.7	—
1960	—	13.6	13.6	11.5	2.1	1.4
1961	—	24.1	24.1	13.7	10.4	8.3
1962	—	25.0	25.0	15.9	9.1	-1.3
1963	2.7	32.6	35.3	20.3	15.0	5.9
1964	14.2	38.1	52.3	28.0	24.3	9.3
1965	25.6	51.9	77.5	36.4	41.1	16.8

[a] Excluding credits against foreign securities pledged with the Bank of Ghana by the Cocoa Marketing Board in 1961 (£G20 million) and 1962 (£G23.7 million).

[b] Since April 1964, other deposits include advance deposits against the establishment of letters of credit.

Sources: *Statistical Year Book*, 1961, tables 135, 136 and 138(a), pp. 124–125.
Statistical Year Book, 1962, tables 139 and 140, p. 139.
Statistical Year Book, 1963, tables 145 and 146, p. 151.
Bank of Ghana Report, June 1960, appendix 6, pp. 22–23.
Bank of Ghana Report, June 1961, table 6, pp. 34–35.
Bank of Ghana Report, June 1964, tables XLV and L, pp. 49 and 60.
Bank of Ghana Report, June 1965, tables XLII and XLVII, pp. 58 and 68.
Bank of Ghana Report, June 1967, tables 5 and 9, pp. 41 and 45.
Worksheets of the Research Department, Bank of Ghana.

Table X. Reserve Requirements for the Commercial Banks
(Effective since 1st April, 1964)

Type of Assets	Reserve Requirements (as % of total deposit liabilities)	
	From 1st March to 31st August	From 1st September to 28th February
1. Cash Reserves:	8	8
a) Cash in tills		
b) Net balances with banks in Ghana		
c) Current account deposits with the Bank of Ghana [a]		
2. Other Liquid Reserves:	40	46
a) Government of Ghana Treasury Bills		
b) Approved agricultural loans		
c) Approved industrial loans		
d) Special cash deposits with the Bank of Ghana ('L' Account) [b]		
3. Special Deposits with the Bank of Ghana ('B' Account) [c]	5	5
4. Government of Ghana Stocks	18	18
Total (1 + 2 + 3 + 4)	71	77

[a] Excluding: i) foreign currency deposits with the Bank of Ghana against sight balances due to banks abroad;
  ii) borrowing from banks abroad; and,
  iii) mandatory advance deposits (of 15%) in respect of letters of credit to finance imports of consumer goods.

[b] Required if the sum of items a, b and c under 2 falls below the required minimum of 40/46%. Amounts held in 'L' Account were originally interest bearing (at a rate 3/4% below the current Bank Rate), but were later on declared to be non-interest bearing.

[c] Represents the minimum amount to be maintained at all times with the Bank of Ghana. Amounts held in 'B' Accounts were also interest bearing (at a rate 3/4% below current Bank Rate), but were later on declared to be non-interest bearing.

Source: Bank of Ghana Report, June 1964, pp. 89–90.

Table XI. **Central Government Consumption Expenditure and Current Transfers to Domestic Sectors, 1958–65**
(£G million)

	1958	1959	1960	1961	1962	1963	1964	1965
Consumption Expenditure:								
1. Wages and salaries (Military and civilian)	16.8	15.2	17.6	22.5	22.2	23.2	25.5	28.1
2. Military expenditure on new machinery and equipment	–	–	1.2	2.4	2.3	2.1	2.1	1.9
3. Other goods and services	11.8	14.7	15.8	19.6	17.9	21.2	25.8	31.7
4. Rent	0.1	0.3	0.2	0.3	0.4	0.3	0.3	0.3
5. Interest on public debt	0.8	0.9	1.4	1.6	2.4	2.7	6.2	7.0
6. Contingencies	–	–	0.2	0.4	0.5	1.0	2.2	2.1
Total	29.5	31.1	36.4	46.8	45.7	50.4	62.2	71.1
Current Transfers to Domestic Sectors:								
1. Statutory corporations and public institutions	5.8	7.7	10.3	13.4	17.9	20.1	24.1	28.0
2. Local governments	1.6	1.7	1.8	2.3	1.3	1.2	1.3	1.6
3. Subsidies	–	–	0.1	0.1	0.2	0.5	2.9	0.2
4. Households	2.4	3.5	4.2	4.7	4.3	4.4	5.5	5.9
Total	9.9	12.9	16.5	20.5	23.7	26.2	33.8	35.7

N.B. Figures do not always add up to totals because of rounding.

Source: Worksheets of the Central Bureau of Statistics.

Table XII. **Central Government Gross Domestic Fixed Investment, 1958—65**

(£G million)

	1958	1959	1960	1961	1962	1963	1964	1965
Direct Investment:								
1. New buildings and construction (Military and civilian)	7.7	12.5	16.2	24.9	23.0	22.3	30.1	38.3
2. New machinery and equipment	0.8	1.4	3.8	8.0	5.9	4.8	8.0	10.0
3. Expenditure on surveys	0.1	0.3	0.3	0.5	1.6	0.7	0.5	1.5
Total	8.6	14.2	20.3	33.4	30.5	27.8	38.6	49.8
Capital Transfers to Domestic Sectors:								
1. Statutory corporations and public institutions	1.6	5.3	4.7	8.1	11.0	17.4	22.1	19.8
2. Local governments	0.9	1.1	0.6	1.4	0.6	0.2	0.2	0.3
3. Private enterprises and households	0.6	0.2	0.3	0.7	0.2	–	–	–
Total	3.1	6.6	5.6	10.2	11.8	17.6	22.3	20.1

Source: Worksheets of the Central Bureau of Statistics.

147

Table XIII. **Loss from Terms of Trade, 1957–65**

	1957	1958	1959	1960	1961	1962	1963	1964	1965
Imports[a] at current prices (£G million)	107.0	95.0	126.0	148.0	163.0	135.0	145.0	141.5	188.0
Imports[a] at 1960 constant prices (£G million)	109.0	97.0	126.5	148.0	161.0	141.0	156.0	136.0	175.0
Loss (− = gain)	−2.0	−2.0	−0.5	0.0	2.0	−6.0	−11.0	5.5	13.0
Exports at current prices (£G million)	96.0	110.0	120.0	123.0	122.0	120.0	117.0	123.5	126.0
Exports at 1960 constant prices (£G million)	107.0	94.0	109.0	123.0	138.0	162.0	154.0	135.5	167.0
Loss (− = gain)	11.0	−16.0	−11.0	0.0	16.0	42.0	37.0	12.0	41.0
Total Loss (− = gain)	9.0	−18.0	−11.5	0.0	18.0	36.0	26.0	17.5	54.0
Index of Import prices (1960 = 100)	98.2	98.0	99.6	100.0	101.2	95.7	93.0	104.0	107.4
Index of Export prices (1960 = 100)	89.7	117.0	110.1	100.0	88.4	74.1	76.0	91.1	75.4
Terms of Trade[b]	91.3	119.4	110.5	100.0	87.4	77.4	81.7	87.6	70.2

[a] Goods and non-factor services, excluding ships and aircrafts.

[b] Ratio of Export prices to import prices.

Source: Derived from appendix table I.

Table XIV. **Central Government Finances, 1957–65** (Calendar years)
(£G million)

	1957	1958	1959	1960	1961	1962	1963	1964	1965
1. Current revenue [a]	54.6	63.4	65.7	68.2	73.4	80.1	87.8	102.0	141.9
2. Current expenditure	41.5	42.4	48.0	58.6	68.2	75.6	82.8	99.0	109.9
3. Current savings (1–2)	13.1	21.0	17.7	9.6	5.2	4.5	5.0	3.0	32.0
4. Capital expenditure	12.4	14.9	22.1	34.4	43.0	50.3	52.4	54.1	71.0
a) Investment	(10.1)	(11.0)	(15.3)	(24.8)	(34.5)	(38.5)	(34.9)	(34.1)	(50.7)
b) Transfers on capital account [b]	(2.3)	(3.9)	(6.8)	(9.6)	(8.5)	(11.8)	(17.5)	(20.0)	(20.3)
5. Deficit (− = surplus) (2 + 4 − 1)	−0.7	−6.1	4.4	24.8	37.8	45.8	47.4	51.1	39.0
6. Current savings as % of capital expenditure	105.4	140.9	80.1	27.9	12.1	9.0	9.5	5.5	45.0
7. Current revenue as % of GNP in current prices	14.9	16.3	14.9	14.4	14.6	14.8	14.8	15.2	17.8
8. Expenditure as % of GNP in current prices	14.7	14.7	15.9	19.7	22.0	23.2	22.7	22.7	22.8
of which: a) current expenditure	(11.3)	(10.9)	(10.9)	(12.4)	(13.5)	(13.9)	(13.9)	(14.7)	(13.8)
b) capital expenditure	(3.4)	(3.8)	(5.0)	(7.3)	(8.5)	(9.3)	(8.8)	(8.0)	(9.0)

[a] Excluding refund of revenue and voluntary contributions from the Cocoa Marketing Board.

[b] Mainly to statutory corporations and public institutions.

N.B. During the period under review, the fiscal year in Ghana was changed twice: in 1962 from July/June to October/September and in 1965 from October/September to January/December. To avoid confusion and for the sake of consistency fiscal years have been converted into calendar years using half-yearly or quarterly averages.

Sources: Derived from the data supplied by the Central Bureau of Statistics and *Financial Statement*, 1960–61, table X, pp. 16–18.

Table XV. **Central Government Current Revenue, 1957–65** (Calendar years)

	1957	1958	1959	1960	1961	1962	1963	1964	1965
Income tax (Company & personal)	5.3	5.7	5.8	6.1	7.8	11.2	13.3	22.5	27.2
Property tax	–	–	–	–	–	0.1	0.2	0.3	0.4
Mineral duty	2.2	2.1	1.7	1.8	1.8	1.7	1.4	1.2	1.3
Import duties	15.7	15.6	17.5	22.4	27.4	30.9	33.9	34.9	53.8
Export duty – Cocoa	17.0	23.5	23.2	18.4	15.0	12.5	13.7	14.0	9.9
Export duties – Others	0.6	0.6	0.8	0.8	0.7	0.5	0.6	0.6	0.4
Excise & local duties	1.2	2.4	2.8	2.8	3.4	4.7	6.6	8.4	10.7
Purchase tax	–	–	–	–	1.4	2.1	2.1	2.2	0.8
Sales tax	–	–	–	–	–	–	–	–	15.8
Sales of goods & services	3.9	4.6	5.5	6.7	7.5	8.1	9.0	10.6	10.5
Rent, interest, profits, fees, fines, licences and grants	8.0	7.9	7.3	8.3					9.0
Betting tax, stamp duties, royalties, entertainment tax, hotel tax, airport tax, foreign travel tax	0.3	0.3	0.3	0.3	8.6	8.4	7.1	7.9	1.4
Miscellaneous (including transfers between government agencies)	0.7	0.8	0.8	0.6					0.8
Total current revenue	54.9	63.5	65.7	68.3	73.6	80.2	87.9	102.1	142.0
Refund of revenue	0.3	0.1	0.0	0.1	0.2	0.1	0.1	0.1	0.1
Net current revenue	54.6	63.4	65.7	68.2	73.4	80.1	87.8	102.0	141.9

(For the years 1961–1964 the last three categories — Rent etc.; Betting tax etc.; and Miscellaneous — are shown as a single combined figure: 8.6, 8.4, 7.1, 7.9 respectively.)

Sources: Calculated by using half-yearly or quarterly averages of the fiscal year data obtained from:

> *Financial Statement*, 1960–1961, table X, p. 18.
> *Financial Statement*, 1962–1963, table VIII, p. 28.
> *Financial Statement*, 1963–1964, table VIII, p. 32.
> *Financial Statement*, 1965, table VIII, p. 39.
> *Financial Statement*, 1966, table VIII, p. 28.
> *Economic Survey*, 1964, tables II and III, pp. 115–116.
> *Financial Statement*, 1967–1968, table VIII, p. 21.

Table XVI. **National Debt, 1959–65** (At the End of Year)
(£G million)

	1959	1960	1961	1962	1963	1964	1965
Internal							
Treasury Bills		6.0	8.0	36.6	36.2	51.7	67.4
Ways and Means Advances		—	—	—	15.0	20.0	20.0
Special Loan from the Bank of Ghana		—	—	—	—	—	12.5
Cocoa Marketing Board Loans		31.1	30.5	29.7	29.0	12.0	10.4
Government Stocks/Bonds		1.5	5.5	5.5	35.0	65.7	78.8
National Development Bonds		—	—	8.8	17.9	12.2	11.9
Ghana Railway and Harbours Administration Loan		—	—	—	—	3.7	3.7
Total Internal Debt	16.5	38.6	44.0	80.6	133.1	165.3	204.7
External							
Government Stocks		3.2	3.2	3.2	1.2	1.2	1.2
I. M. F.		—	—	5.1	5.1	5.1	3.1
Joint Consolidated and Miscellaneous Funds		—	7.1	3.6	4.5	5.5	5.7
Volta River Project Loan		—	—	—	6.1	16.1	22.5
Counterpart Funds		—	—	—	—	3.4	3.9
Suppliers' Credits		13.8	28.4	60.8	60.8	156.9	183.9
Total External Debt	6.0	17.0	38.7	72.7	77.7	188.2	220.3
Total National Debt	22.5	55.6	82.7	153.3	210.8	353.5	425.0
Debt Charges (including amortization)	n.a.	n.a.	n.a.	2.7	4.3	8.8	22.4
Debt Charges as %₀ of Export Earnings	n.a.	n.a.	n.a.	2.4	4.0	7.7	19.5
Debt Charges as %₀ of Government Current Revenue	n.a.	n.a.	n.a.	3.4	4.9	8.6	15.8

N.B. Breakdown for 1959 is not available.

Sources: *Economic Survey,* 1964, table 8, p. 30.
Bank of Ghana Report, June 1966, table 12, p. 57.
Bank of Ghana Report, June 1967, table 11, p. 48.

Selected Bibliography

A. General

1. AHRENSDORF, Joachim, 'Central Banking Policies and Inflation: A Case Study of Four Less Developed Economies', I.M.F. *Staff Papers,* Vol. VII, 1959–60, pp. 274–301.
2. ANGEL, J. W., 'The Components of the Circular Velocity of Money', *The Quarterly Journal of Economics,* Vol. 51, No. 2, February, 1937, pp. 224–72.
3. BADGER, Doland G., 'The Balance of Payments: A Tool of Economic Analysis', I.M.F. *Staff Papers,* Vol. II, 1951–52, pp. 86–197.
4. BALL, R. J., *Inflation and the Theory of Money,* George Allen and Unwin Ltd., London, 1964.
5. BARAN, Paul A., *The Political Economy of Growth,* Prometheus Paper Back, 1960.
6. BERNSTEIN, E. M. and PATEL, I. G., 'Inflation in Relation to Economic Development', I.M.F. *Staff Papers,* Vol. II, 1951–52, pp. 363–98. Reprinted in *Studies in Economic Development* (Eds. Bernard Okun and Richard W. Richardson), Holt, Rinehart and Winston, Inc., New York, 1965, pp. 433–48.
7. BERNSTEIN, E. M., 'General Problems of Financing Development Programmes', *Journal of Finance,* Vol. XII, May 1957, pp. 167–77.
8. BIRD, Richard and OLDMAN, Olivar (Eds.), *Readings on Taxation in Developing Countries,* The Johns Hopkins Press, Baltimore, 1964.
9. BROWN, A. J., *The Great Inflation 1939–51,* Oxford University Press, London, 1955.
10. BUCHANAN, James M., *Public Principles of Public Debt,* Richard D. Irwin, Inc., Illinois, 1958.
11. BUCHANAN, James M., *The Public Finances,* Richard D. Irwin, Inc., Illinois, 1958.
12. CAIRNCROSS, A. K., *Factors in Economic Development,* George Allen and Unwin Ltd., London, 1962.
13. CHELLIAH, Raj J., *Fiscal Policy in Underdeveloped Countries,* George Allen and Unwin Ltd., London, 1960.
14. CRICK, W. F., 'The Genesis of Bank Deposits', *Economica,* Vol. 7 (1927), pp. 191–202. Reprinted in *Readings in Monetary Theory,* AEA Series, George Allen and Unwin Ltd., London, 1956, pp. 41–53.
15. DAY, A. C. L., *Outline of Monetary Economics,* Oxford University Press, London, 1960.
16. DIAMOND, Marcus, 'Trends in the Flow of International Private Capital, 1957–65', I.M.F. *Staff Papers,* Vol. XIV, 1967, pp. 1–42.
17. DUE, John F., *Taxation and Economic Development in Tropical Africa,* The M.I.T. Press, Cambridge, Massachusetts, 1963.
18. Economic Commission for Asia and the Far East (ECAFE), 'Deficit Financing for Economic Development', *Economic Bulletin for Asia and the Far East,* Vol. V (November 1954), pp. 1–18.

19. ELLIS, H. S., 'Some Fundamentals in the Theory of Velocity', *Readings in Monetary Theory*, AEA Series, George Allen and Unwin Ltd., London, 1956, pp. 89–128.

20. FRIEDMAN, Milton, *Essays in Positive Economics*, University of Chicago Press, Chicago, 1953.

21. FRIEDMAN, Milton (Ed.), *Studies in the Quantity Theory of Money*, University of Chicago Press, Chicago, 1956.

22. FRIEDMAN, Milton, *A Programme for Monetary Stability*, Fordham University Press, New York, 1960.

23. GHOSH, S., *Inflation in An Underdeveloped Economy: A Study of Inflation in India*, World Press, Calcutta, 1959.

24. Government of India, *The Second Five-Year Plan*, 1956.

25. Government of Pakistan, *The Second Five-Year Plan*, (1960–65), June 1960.

26. GURLEY, John G. and SHAW, Edward S., *Money in a Theory of Finance*, The Brooklings Institution, Washington D.C., 1966.

27. HANSEN, Bent, *Theory of Inflation*, George Allen and Unwin Ltd., London, 1951.

28. HANSEN, Bent, *The Economic Theory of Fiscal Policy*, George Allen and Unwin Ltd., London, 1958.

29. HAQ, Mahbubul, *Deficit Financing in Pakistan, 1951–60*, The Institute of Development Economics, Karachi, 1961.

30. HASAN, Parvez, *Deficit Financing and Capital Formation, The Pakistan Experience, 1951–59*, The Institute of Development Economics, Karachi, 1962.

31. HAWKINS, E. K., 'The Growth of a Money Economy in Nigeria and Ghana', *Oxford Economic Papers*, Vol. 10, No. 3, (October 1958), pp. 339–54.

32. HICKS, U. K., *Development Finance – Planning and Control*, Oxford University Press, Oxford, 1965.

33. HIRSCHMAN, Albert O., *The Strategy of Economic Development*, Yale University Press, New Haven and London, 1958.

34. HORSEFIELD, J. Keith, 'The Measurement of Inflation', I.M.F. *Staff Papers*, Vol. I, 1950–51, pp. 17–48.

35. JUCKER-FLEETWOOD, Erin E., *Money and Finance in Africa*, George Allen and Unwin Ltd., London, 1964.

36. KALDOR, Nicholas, 'Economic Growth and the Problem of Inflation', *Economica*, Vol. XXVI, No. 103 and 104 (1959), pp. 212–26 and 287–98.

37. KAMARCK, Andrew M., *The Economics of African Development*, Pall Mall, London, 1967.

38. KURIHARA, Kenneth K., *Monetary Theory and Public Policy*, George Allen and Unwin Ltd., London, 1965.

39. LERNER, A. P., *Economics of Employment*, McGraw-Hill, New York, 1951.

40. LEWIS, W. Arthur, *The Theory of Economic Growth*, George Allen and Unwin Ltd., London, 1963.

41. LEWIS, W. Arthur, *Some Aspects of Economic Development*, University of Ghana, Accra, 1969.

42. LUNDBERG, Erik, *Studies in the Theory of Economic Expansion*, Basil Blackwell, Oxford, 1955.

43. MYINT, H., *The Economics of the Developing Countries*, Hutchinson & Co., London, 1965.

44. NEWLYN, W. T., *Theory of Money*, Oxford University Press, Oxford, 1962.

45. NEVIN, Edward, *Capital Funds in Underdeveloped Countries*, Macmillan & Co., London, 1963.

46. NURKSE, Ragnar, *Problems of Capital Formation in Underdeveloped Countries,* Basil Blackwell, Oxford, 1964.

47. Organization for Economic Co-operation and Development (OECD), *The Inflow of Financial Resources to Less-Developed Countries, 1961–65,* Paris, 1967.

48. Organization for European Economic Co-operation (OEEC), *Statistics of Sources and Uses of Finance,* Paris, 1960.

49. PATEL, I. G., 'Selective Credit Controls in Underdeveloped Economies', I.M.F. *Staff Papers,* Vol. IV, 1954–55, pp. 73–84.

50. PATTERSON, Gardner, 'Impact of Deficit Financing in Underdeveloped Countries: Some Neglected Aspects', *Journal of Finance,* Vol. XII, No. 2, (May 1957), pp. 179–89.

51. PREBISCH, Raul, 'Economic Development or Monetary Stability: The False Dilemma', *Economic Bulletin for Latin America,* Vol. VI, No. 1, (March 1961).

52. PREST, A. R., *Public Finance in Underdeveloped Countries,* Weidenfeld and Nicolson, London, 1962.

53. RAO, V. K. R. V., 'Investment Income and the Multiplier in An Underdeveloped Economy', *Indian Economic Review,* February, 1952. Reprinted in *The Economics of Underdevelopment* (Eds. A. N. Agarwala and S. P. Singh), Oxford University Press, New York, 1963, pp. 205–18.

54. RAO, V. K. R. V., 'Deficit Financing, Capital Formation and Price Behaviour in An Underdeveloped Economy', *Indian Economic Review,* February 1953, pp. 55–91.

55. ROBINSON, Joan, *Economic Philosophy,* Penguin Books Ltd., 1964.

56. SCHATZ, S. P., 'Inflation in Underdeveloped Areas: A Theoretical Analysis', *The American Economic Review,* Vol. XLVII (1957), pp. 571–93.

57. SCHUMPETER, Joseph A., *The Theory of Economic Development,* Oxford University Press, New York, 1961.

58. SEERS, Dudley, 'A Theory of Inflation and Growth in Underdeveloped Countries Based on the Experience of Latin America', *Oxford Economic Papers,* Vol. 14, No. 2, 1962, pp. 174–95.

59. SEN, S. N., *Central Banking in Underdeveloped Money Markets,* Bookland Ltd., Calcutta, 1952.

60. SINGER, H. W., 'Deficit Financing of Public Capital Formation', *Social and Economic Studies,* Special Number, 1958, pp. 91–96.

61. STOLPER, Wolfgang F., *Planning Without Facts,* Harvard University Press, Cambridge, Massachusetts, 1966.

62. WHITE, William H., 'Measuring the Inflationary Significance of a Government Budget', I.M.F. *Staff Papers,* Vol. I, 1950–51, pp. 355–78.

B. Ghana

I. Books

1. AFRIFA, A. A., *The Ghana Coup,* Frank Cass and Co. Ltd., London, 1966.

2. BIRMINGHAM, W., NEUSTADT, I. and OMABOE, E. N., (Eds.), *A Study of Contemporary Ghana, Vol. One – The Economy of Ghana,* George Allen and Unwin Ltd., London, 1966.

3. NKRUMAH, Kwame, *The Dark Days in Ghana,* Lawrence and Wishart, London, 1968.

4. SZERESZEWSKI, R., *Structural Changes in the Economy of Ghana, 1891–1911,* Weidenfeld and Nicolson, London, 1965.

II. Articles

1. AGAMA, G. KPORTUFU, 'The Growth of Money and Public Debt in Ghana, 1957–65', *The Economic Bulletin of Ghana,* Vol. XII, No. 1 (1968), pp. 8–33.
2. AHMAD, Naseem, 'Public Finance and Fiscal Policy in Ghana', *Supplementary Readings in Economics,* Series A, No. 3, Legon, 1964 (Mimeographed).
3. AHMAD, Naseem, 'Why Import Controls?', *Audit Bulletin,* Vol. VI, No. 10 (1964), pp. 1–8.
4. AHMAD, Naseem, 'Some Aspects of Budgetary Policy in Ghana', *The Economic Bulletin of Ghana,* Vol. X, No. 1 (1966), pp. 3–22.
5. AHMAD, Naseem, 'Financing of Government Activity in Ghana, 1957–65', *Supplementary Readings in Economics,* Series A, No. 10, Legon, 1968 (Mimeographed).
6. AHMAD, Naseem, 'Income Taxation in Ghana', *Supplementary Readings in Economics,* Series A, No. 11, Legon, 1968, (Mimeographed).
7. ANDIC, F. and ANDIC, S., 'A Survey of Ghana's Tax System and Finances', *Public Finance,* Vol. XVIII, No. 1 (1963), pp. 5–45.
8. BIRMINGHAM, W., 'The Economic Development of Ghana', *Planning and Growth in Rich and Poor Countries* (Eds. W. Birmingham and A. G. Ford), George Allen and Unwin Ltd., London, 1966, pp. 172–94.
9. BISSUE, Isaac, 'Ghana's Seven-Year Development Plan in Retrospect', *The Economic Bulletin of Ghana,* Vol. XI, No. 1 (1967), pp. 21–44.
10. ESHAG, Eprime and RICHARDS, P. J., 'A Comparison of Economic Developments in Ghana and the Ivory Coast since 1960', *Bulletin,* Oxford University Institute of Economics and Statistics, Vol. 29, No. 4 (November 1967), pp. 353–72.
11. FRIMPONG-ANSAH, J. H., 'Monetary Projections in Ghana', *The Economic Bulletin of Ghana,* Vol. IX, No. 3 & 4 (1965), pp. 3–13.
12. KILLICK, Tony, 'The Performance of Ghana's Economy: 1963 and After', *The Economic Bulletin of Ghana,* Vol. IX, No. 1 (1965), pp. 24–45.
13. KILLICK, A. and SZERESZEWSKI, R., 'The Economy of Ghana', *The Economics of Africa,* (Eds. P. Robson and D. A. Lury), George Allen and Unwin Ltd., London, 1969, pp. 79–126.
14. LAWSON, Rowena M., 'Inflation in the Consumer Market in Ghana', *The Economic Bulletin of Ghana,* Vol. X, No. 1 (1966) pp. 36–51.
15. NORRIS, Robert W., 'On Inflation in Ghana', *Financing African Development,* (Ed. Tom J. Farer), The M.I.T. Press, Cambridge, Massachusetts, 1965, pp. 94–109.
16. OFORI-ATTA, Jones, 'Some Aspects of Economic Policy in Ghana, 1957–61', *The Economic Bulletin of Ghana,* Vol. XI, No. 3 (1967), pp. 35–53.
17. ORD, H. W., 'Agricultural Commodity Projections in Ghana', *The Economic Bulletin of Ghana,* Vol. IX, No. 3 & 4 (1965), pp. 14–20.
18. RIMMER, Douglas, 'The Crisis in the Ghana Economy', *Journal of Modern African Studies,* Vol. IV, No. 1 (1966), pp. 17–32.
19. STOCES, Ferdinand, 'Agricultural Production in Ghana, 1955–65', *The Economic Bulletin of Ghana,* Vol. X, No. 3 (1966), pp. 3–32.

III. Official Publications and Reports

1. Bank of Ghana, *Reports of the Board of Directors,* (Annual), 1959/60 to 1967/68.
2. Bank of Ghana, Research Department, *Quarterly Economic Bulletins,* Vol. 3, No. 1, 2 and 3 (1963), Vol. 5, No. 1 and 2 (March and June, 1965), Vol. 8, No. 4 (Oct. – Dec. 1968), Vol. 9, No. 1 and 2 (1969).

155

3. *Bank of Ghana Act, 1963.*
4. Central Bureau of Statistics, *Economic Surveys,* (Annual), 1960 to 1967.
5. Central Bureau of Statistics, *Statistical Year Books,* (Annual), 1961 to 1964.
6. Central Bureau of Statistics, *Quarterly Digest of Statistics,* Vol. XII to XVI (1963 to 1967).
7. *For Work and Happiness, Programme of the Convention People's Party,* 1962.
8. *Ghana's Economy and Aid Requirements in 1967,* May 1967.
9. Planning Commission, *Seven-Year Plan for National Reconstruction and Development, 1963/64–1969/70.*
10. Planning Commission, *Annual Plan for the Second Plan Year (1965 Financial Year).*
11. *Two-Year Development Plan – From Stabilization to Development, (A Plan for the period Mid-1968 to Mid-1970),* July 1968.
12. Ministry of Agriculture, Division of Agricultural Economics and Statistics, *Agricultural Census,* Phase II, Vol. I.
13. *The Financial Statements,* 1956/57 to 1963/64, 1966, and 1966/67 to 1968/69.
14. *1963–64 Budget Statement* (22nd October, 1963).
15. *The Budget 1965.*
16. *1965 Budget – Analysis and Salient Points.*
17. *1965 Supplementary Budget Statement* (10th September, 1965)
18. *Sales Tax Act, 1965* (Act 257)
19. *1966 Budget Statement* (22nd February, 1966).
20. *Budget Statements* for 1966/67 to 1969/70.
21. *The Budget 1966/67.*
22. *Report of the Commission of Enquiry into Trade Malpractices in Ghana,* (The Abraham Commission Report), August, 1965.
23. *Report on the Administration and Operation of State Enterprises Under the Work Schedule of the State Enterprises Secretariat for the Period 1964–65,* September 1966 (Mimeographed).
24. *Report and Financial Statements by the Accountant-General and Report thereon by the Auditor-General for the year ended 31st December, 1964;* 1967.
25. *Outline of Government Economic Policy,* August, 1967.
26. U.S. Department of Agriculture, *Projected Level of Demand, Supply and Imports of Agricultural Products in 1965, 1970 and 1975* (in Ghana), Edinburgh, 1964.
27. WALTERS, Dorothy, *Report on the National Accounts of Ghana, 1955–61,* (Walters Report), Accra, 1962 (Typescript).

Studies within the African Research Programme
of the
Ifo-Institut für Wirtschaftsforschung, Munich

Published: **A. In the series "Afrika-Studien"**

(No. 1–18 by Springer-Verlag, Berlin – Heidelberg – New York; No. 19 ff. by Weltforum-Verlag, Munich)

No. 1   **Development Banks and Corporations in Tropical Africa**
By Naseem Ahmad and Ernst Becher, 1964, 86 pages, in German

No. 2   **Agricultural Development in Tanganyika**
By Hans Ruthenberg, 1964, 212 pages, in English

No. 3   **National Accounting Systems in Tropical Africa**
By Rolf Güsten and Helmut Helmschrott, 1965, 69 pages, in German

No. 4   **Contributions to Internal Migration
and Population Development in Liberia**
By Hans W. Jürgens, 1965, 104 pages, in German

No. 5   **Annotated Bibliography of Social Research in East Africa
1954—1963**
By Angela von Molnos, 1965, 304 pages, in German

No. 6   **The Political and Economic Role of the Asian Minority
in East Africa**
By Indira Rothermund, 1965, 75 pages, in German

No. 7   **Land Tenure Reform in Kenya**
By Hanfried Fliedner, 1965, 136 pages, in German

No. 8   **Taxation and Economic Development in East Africa**
By Lübbe Schnittger, 1966, 216 pages, in German

No. 9   **Problems of Economic Growth and Planning:
The Sudan Example**
By Rolf Güsten, 1966, 74 pages, in English

No. 10   **African Agricultural Production Development Policy
in Kenya 1952—1965**
By Hans Ruthenberg, 1966, 180 pages, in English

No. 11   **Land Use and Animal Husbandry in Sukumaland/Tanzania**
By Dietrich von Rotenhan, 1966, 131 pages, in German

To be published:

No. 59   Studies in Zebu Cattle Breeding in Tropical Africa
         By R. Bartha (in German with an English Summary)

B. In the African Studies special series "Information and Documentation"

Published:

No. 1   Africa-Vademecum (basic data on the economic structure and
        development of Africa)
        Prepared by F. Betz, 1968, 163 pages, in German, with additional
        headings in English and French
No. 2   Development Banks and Institutions in Africa
        By H. Harlander and D. Mezger, 1969, 211 pages, in German
No. 3   Development Aid to Africa
        By F. Betz, 1970, 120 pages, in German

C. As mimeographs (African Research Reports)

Published:

(early editions can be obtained through the African Studies Centre of the
Ifo Institute for Economic Research; the more recent editions (from 1968
onwards) are available through the Weltforum-Verlag, Munich).

Economic Planning and Development Policy in Tropical Africa
By N. Ahmad, E. Becher and E. Harder, 1965, 283 pages, in German
(out of print)

The Human Factor in the Development of the Kilombero Valley
By O. Raum, 1965, 56 pages, in English (out of print)

The EEC Market Regulations for Agricultural Products and their
Implications for Developing Countries
By H. Klemm and P. v. Marlin, 1965, 95 pages, in German (out of print)

The Impact of External Economic Relations on the Economic
Development of East Africa
By P. v. Marlin, 1966, 110 pages, in English (out of print)

Crop Cultivation on the Island of Madagascar with Special Reference to
Rice Growing
By Alfred H. Rabe, 1965, 346 pages, in German (out of print)

Economic Research in Tropical Africa. Results of an Informatory Trip
to Egypt, Ethiopia, Kenya, Uganda, Tanzania, Malawi, Zambia, Congo
(Kinshasa), Nigeria, Ghana and Senegal in April and May 1966
By Hildegard Harlander, 1966, 193 pages, in German

Israeli Aid to Developing Countries with Special Reference to East Africa
By F. Goll, 1967, 189 pages, in German

The Economy of South West Africa (a Study in Economic Geography)
By Axel J. Halbach, 1967, 210 pages, in German (out of print)

Co-operative Farming in Kenya and Tanzania
By Nikolaus Newiger, 1967, 157 pages, in English (out of print)

Game Protection and Game Utilization in Rhodesia and in South Africa
By Wolfgang Erz, 1967, 97 pages, in German (out of print)

Zoological Studies in the Kivu Region (Congo-Kinshasa)
By Fritz Dieterlen and Peter Kunkel, 1967, 138 pages, in German

Recent English Economic Research in East Africa. A Selected Bibliography
By Dorothea Mezger and Eleonore Littich, 1967, 383 pages, in German (out of print)

The Attitude of Various Tribes of the Republic of Togo, Especially the Ewe on the Plateau de Dayes, towards the Problem of Commissioned Cattle Herding by the Fulbe (Peulh) of West Africa
By Julius O. Müller, 1967, 187 pages, in French

Examination of the Physical Development of Tanzanian Youth
By H. W. Jürgens, 1967, 152 pages, in English

The Chemical and Allied Industries in Kenya
By Hans Reichelt, 1967, 182 pages, in English

Traditional Farming and Land Development in the Kilombero Valley/Tanzania
By Eckhard Baum, 1967, 150 pages, in German

The Organization of Milk Markets in East Africa
By Helmut Klemm, 1967, 164 pages, in German

Botanical Investigations in the Masai Country/Tanzania (an Example from the Semi-Arid Areas of East Africa)
By H. Leippert, 1968, 184 pages, in German

Evaluation of Aerial Photography in East Africa (an Inventory)
By K. Gerresheim, 1968, 225 pages, in German

Manufacturing and Processing Industries in Tanzania
By K. Schädler, 1969, 55 pages, in English

Agricultural Development in Malawi
By H. Dequin, 1969, 248 pages, in English

Development Aid to Africa – with Special Reference to the Countries of East Africa
By K. Erdmann, 1969, 186 pages, in German

Vegetable Cultivation in Tropical Highlands: the Kigezi Example (Uganda)
By F. Scherer, 1969, 227 pages, in English

Science and Development Policy. The Problem of Applying Research Results
By M. Bohnet, 1969, 35 pages, in German

Importance, Volume, Forms and Development Possibilities of Private Saving in East Africa
By G. Hübner, 1970, 343 pages, in German

Operational Concepts of the Infrastructure in the Economic Development Process, 1970, 203 pages, in German
By H. Amann, 1970, 203 pages, in German

Problems of the Transport Economy in Tanzania with Special Reference to Road Transport
By R. Hofmeier, 1970, 467 pages, in German

Beef Production in East Africa
By K. Meyn, 1970, in English

The Distribution of Income and Education in Kenya: Causes and Potential Political Consequences
By D. Berg-Schlosser, 1970, 80 Pages (in English)

D. In preparation:

The Present State of Legislation in East Africa
By G. Spreen

Development Possibilities of the Pig and Poultry Industry in East Africa
By H. Späth

Comparative Investigations into the Efficiency of Utilizable Ruminants in Kenya
By Walter/Dennig

Farm Management Systems in Kenya
By v. Haugwitz/Thorwart

The Influence of Urbanization upon the Development of Rural Areas — with Special Reference to Jinja (Uganda) and Its Surroundings
By Gerken/Schubert/Brandt

The Interrelationship between Man, Nature and Economy: the Example of Madagascar
By W. Marquardt

Applied Research in East Africa and Its Influence on Economic Development
By M. Bohnet and H. Reichelt (in English)

Co-operatives in the Sudan: Their Characteristics, Functions and Suitability in the Socio-Economic Development Process
By M. Bardeleben

Mining and Regional Development in East Africa
By T. Möller

The Economico-Geographical Pattern of East Africa
By K. Engelhard

Iraqw Highland/Tanzania: Resource Analysis of an East African Highland and its Margins
By J. Schultz (in English)

Methods and Problems of Farm Management Surveys in Africa South of the Sahara
By H. Thorwart

The Mau-Mau Movement: Its Socio-Economic and Political Causes and Implications upon British Colonial Policy in Kenya and Africa
By J. Muriuki (in English)

The Requirements for the Means of Transport in East Africa with a View to the Economic Expansion of these Countries
By H. Milbers

Population Trends and Migration in Malawi with Special Reference to the Central Region of Lake Malawi
By U. Weyl

Population Trends in Kenya and Their Implications for Social Services in Rural and Urban Areas
By M. Meck (in English)

Education's Contribution to Economic Development of a Tropical Agrarian Country — the Example of Tanzania
By H. Desselberger

Agrarian Patterns in Ethiopia and their Implications for Economic Growth
By V. Janssen

Problems and Structure of African Smallholder Coffee Plantations in the Highland of Angola
By H. Pössinger

Trypanosomiasis among Man and Animals in Africa — Measures of Control from an Economic Point of View
By H. Jahnke / A. Matteucci

Agricultural Development in the Bantu-Homelands of South and South-West Africa
By W. Magura (in German)

The Sahara and its Margins. Characteristics of a large Natural Region. 3 Volumes.
By H. Schiffers (in German)